Modern Middle East Nations
AND THEIR STRATEGIC PLACE IN THE WORLD

SYRIA

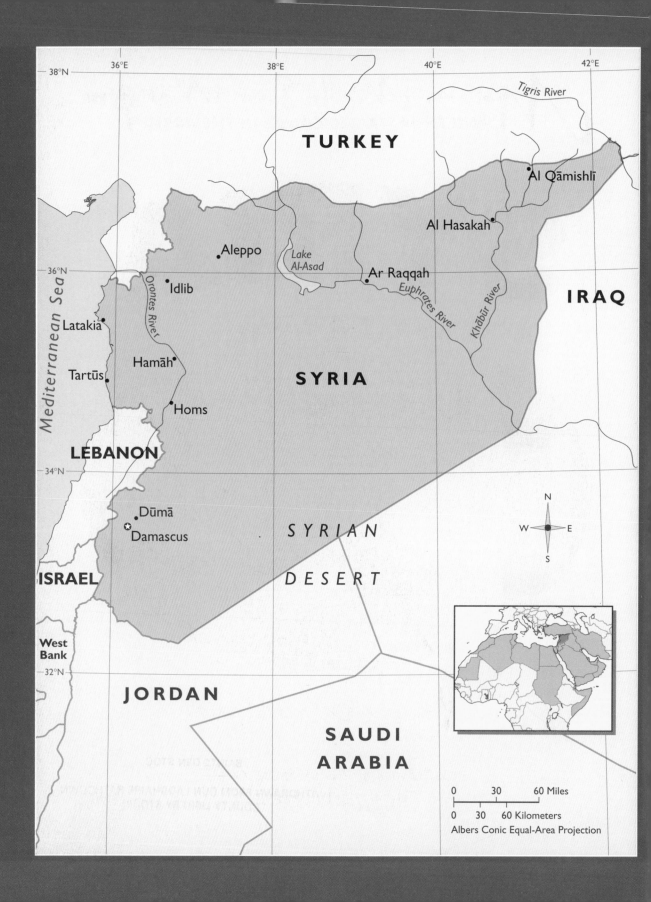

38°N

36°E   38°E   40°E   42°E

Tigris River

TURKEY

Al Qāmishlī

Al Hasakah

Aleppo

Lake
Al-Asad

36°N

Idlib

Ar Raqqah

Orontes River

Euphrates River

Khābūr River

IRAQ

Latakia

Mediterranean Sea

Hamāh

SYRIA

Tartūs

Homs

LEBANON

34°N

N

Dūmā

W   E

Damascus

S Y R I A N

S

ISRAEL

D E S E R T

West
Bank

32°N

JORDAN

**SAUDI
ARABIA**

0   30   60 Miles

0   30   60 Kilometers

Albers Conic Equal-Area Projection

Modern Middle East Nations
AND THEIR STRATEGIC PLACE IN THE WORLD

SYRIA

ANNE MARIE SULLIVAN

MASON CREST PUBLISHERS
PHILADELPHIA

Produced by OTTN Publishing, Stockton, New Jersey

Mason Crest Publishers
370 Reed Road
Broomall, PA 19008
www.masoncrest.com

3 5 7 9 8 6 4 2

Library of Congress Cataloging-in-Publication Data

Sullivan, Anne Marie.
   Syria / Anne Marie Sullivan.
     p. cm. — (Modern Middle East nations and their strategic place in the world)
  Summary: Discusses the geography, history, economy, government, religion, people, foreign
relations, and major cities of Syria.
  Includes bibliographical references and index.
    ISBN 1-59084-506-4
  1. Syria—Juvenile literature.   [1. Syria.]   I. Title. II. Series.
DS93.S82 2003 956.91—dc21

                   2002013008

TABLE OF CONTENTS

Modern Middle East Nations
AND THEIR STRATEGIC PLACE IN THE WORLD

ALGERIA
BAHRAIN
DJIBOUTI
EGYPT
IRAN
IRAQ
ISRAEL
JORDAN
KUWAIT
LEBANON
LIBYA
MAURITANIA
MOROCCO
OMAN
THE PALESTINIANS
QATAR
SAUDI ARABIA
SOMALIA
SUDAN
SYRIA
TUNISIA
TURKEY
UNITED ARAB EMIRATES
YEMEN
THE MIDDLE EAST: FACTS AND FIGURES

Dr. Harvey Sicherman, president and director of the Foreign Policy Research Institute, is the author of such books as *America the Vulnerable: Our Military Problems and How to Fix Them* (2002) and *Palestinian Autonomy, Self-Government and Peace* (1993).

Introduction

by Dr. Harvey Sicherman

Situated as it is between Africa, Europe, and the Far East, the Middle East has played a unique role in world history. Often described as the birthplace of religions (notably Judaism, Christianity, and Islam) and the cradle of civilizations (Egypt, Mesopotamia, Persia), this region and its peoples have given humanity some of its most precious possessions. At the same time, the Middle East has had more than its share of conflicts. The area is strewn with the ruins of fortifications and the cemeteries of combatants, not to speak of modern arsenals for war.

Today, more than ever, Americans are aware that events in the Middle East can affect our security and prosperity. The United States has a considerable military, political, and economic presence throughout much of the region. Developments there regularly find their way onto the front pages of our newspapers and the screens of our television sets.

Still, it is fair to say that most Middle Eastern countries remain a mystery, their cultures and religions barely known, their peoples and politics confusing and strange. The purpose of this book series is to change that, to educate the reader in the basic facts about the 23 states and many peoples that make up the region. (For our purpose, the Middle East also includes the North African states linked by ethnicity, language, and religion to the Arabs, as well as Somalia and Mauritania, which are African but share the Muslim religion and are members of the Arab League.) A notable feature of the series is the integration of geography, demography, and history; economics and politics; culture and religion. The careful student will learn much that he or she needs to know about ever so important lands.

A few general observations are in order as an introduction to the subject matter.

The first has to do with history and politics. The modern Middle East is full of ancient sites and peoples who trace their lineage and literature to antiquity. Many commentators also attribute the Middle East's political conflicts to grievances and rivalries from the distant past. While history is often invoked, the truth is that the modern Middle East political system dates only from the 1920s and was largely created by the British and the French, the victors of World War I. Such states as Algeria, Iraq, Israel, Jordan, Kuwait, Saudi Arabia, Syria, Turkey, and the United Arab Emirates did not exist before 1914—they became independent between 1920 and 1971. Others, such as Egypt and Iran, were dominated by outside powers until well after World War II. Before 1914, most of the region's states were either controlled by the Turkish-run Ottoman Empire or owed allegiance to the Ottoman sultan. (The sultan was also the caliph or highest religious authority in Islam, in the line of the prophet Muhammad's successors, according to the beliefs of the majority of Muslims known as the *Sunni*.) It was this imperial Muslim system that was ended by the largely British military victory over the Ottomans in World War I. Few of the leaders who emerged in the wake of this event were happy with the territories they were assigned or the borders, which were often drawn by Europeans. Yet, the system has endured despite many efforts to change it.

The second observation has to do with economics, demography, and natural resources. The Middle Eastern peoples live in a region of often dramatic geographical contrasts: vast parched deserts and high mountains, some with year-round snow; stone-hard volcanic rifts and lush semi-tropical valleys; extremely dry and extremely wet conditions, sometimes separated by only a few miles; large permanent rivers and wadis, riverbeds dry as a bone until winter rains send torrents of flood from the mountains to the sea. In ancient times, a very skilled agriculture made the Middle East the breadbasket of the Roman Empire, and its trade carried luxury fabrics, foods, and spices both East and West.

Most recently, however, the Middle East has become more known for a single commodity—oil, which is unevenly distributed and largely concentrated in the Persian Gulf and Arabian Peninsula (although large pockets are also to be found in Algeria, Libya, and other sites). There are also new, potentially lucrative offshore gas fields in the Eastern Mediterranean.

This uneven distribution of wealth has been compounded by demographics. Birth rates are very high, but the countries with the most oil are often lightly populated. Over the last decade, Middle East populations under the age of 20 have grown enormously. How will these young people be educated? Where will they work? The failure of most governments in the region to give their people skills and jobs (with notable exceptions such as Israel) has also contributed to large out-migrations. Many have gone to Europe; many others work in other Middle Eastern countries, supporting their families from afar.

Another unsettling situation is the heavy pressure both people and industry have put on vital resources. Chronic water shortages plague the region. Air quality, public sanitation, and health services in the big cities are also seriously overburdened. There are solutions to these problems, but they require a cooperative approach that is sorely lacking.

A third important observation is the role of religion in the Middle East. Americans, who take separation of church and state for granted, should know that most countries in the region either proclaim their countries to be Muslim or allow a very large role for that religion in public life. Among those with predominantly Muslim populations, Turkey alone describes itself as secular and prohibits avowedly religious parties in the political system. Lebanon was a Christian-dominated state, and Israel continues to be a Jewish state. While both strongly emphasize secular politics, religion plays an enormous role in culture, daily life, and legislation. It is also important to recall that Islamic law (*Sharia*) permits people to practice Judaism and Christianity in Muslim states but only as *Dhimmi*, protected but very second-class citizens.

Fourth, the American student of the modern Middle East will be impressed by the varieties of one-man, centralized rule, very unlike the workings of Western democracies. There are monarchies, some with traditional methods of consultation for tribal elders and even ordinary citizens, in Saudi Arabia and many Gulf States; kings with limited but still important parliaments (such as in Jordan and

Morocco); and military and civilian dictatorships, some (such as Syria) even operating on the hereditary principle (Hafez al Assad's son Bashar succeeded him). Turkey is a practicing democracy, although a special role is given to the military that limits what any government can do. Israel operates the freest democracy, albeit constricted by emergency regulations (such as military censorship) due to the Arab-Israeli conflict.

In conclusion, the MODERN MIDDLE EAST NATIONS series will engage imagination and interest simply because it covers an area of such great importance to the United States. Americans may be relative latecomers to the affairs of this region, but our involvement there will endure. We at the Foreign Policy Research Institute hope that these books will kindle a lifelong interest in the fascinating and significant Middle East.

The morning light shines over the ruins of the temple of Baal in Palmyra, Syria. To people living in the region, Syria is known as the "land where the sun rises."

Place in the World

The Syrian Arab Republic lies in the heart of one of the most troubled regions in the world today. This discord stems primarily from the ongoing opposition between Israelis and the region's Arab nations. Since the creation of Israel more than 50 years ago, Syria has had its own troubled relationship with its neighbor to the southwest. One source of conflict is the Golan Heights, a region located on the border between Israel and Syria. Israel captured the Golan Heights in the Six-Day War of 1967, and today Syrians still claim it is rightfully theirs. Over the course of many skirmishes and wars, Israel and its Arab neighbors have made various stabs at peace, but Syria's bitterness toward its neighbor still festers. The nations of this part of the world are struggling to end the decades of bloodshed and find a way to live together in peace. Syria's government remains determined to make peace only on its own terms.

The Middle East is a region situated between Europe to the west, China and India to the east, and Africa to the south. As the cradle of ancient civilization, the Middle East commanded the world's attention long before the modern Arab-Israeli crisis began. Syria, one of the oldest entities of the region, rests on the far eastern shore of the Mediterranean Sea in an area sometimes called the Levant, a French word meaning "sunrise."

To people in the Mediterranean region, the day dawns over Syria. And in many ways, the world we know today also dawned in the ancient geographical Syria, or Greater Syria, as historians call it. Before the European victors of World War I divided up much of the Middle East, Syria encompassed an area covering the present-day states of Syria and Lebanon, as well as the northern parts of Saudi Arabia and Jordan and much of Israel. The modern state of Syria is less than two-thirds the size of Greater Syria.

This region was the site of much of the ancient world's traffic, as travelers frequently passed through going from one place to another. This position at the world's crossroads deeply influenced Syria's history and culture. Today, the remains of Syria's rich and glorious past can be seen in the ruins and archaeological sites throughout the country, which reveal layer after layer of civilization. Some Muslim mosques used in Syria today were built on the foundations of Christian churches. A number of these churches were built on top of Roman temples, some of which were built on the sacred sites of ancient pagan religions.

The seventh century brought a group of Arabians advancing north to Syria. They conquered the Middle East in their passionate zeal to spread their new religion, Islam. A few Syrians are descended from these Arabian tribes; a much larger group descends from the Hittites and various Semitic peoples living in the area before the Arab conquest. Today, Arabs live in many countries in the Middle East and across North Africa. They generally identify themselves not as descendants of Arabian people, but as people who speak the Arabic language and have adopted Arab ways and customs. The cornerstone of Arab culture is the Islamic faith; however, not all Arabs are Muslims, a fact demonstrated by the number of Syrian Christians who continue to practice their faith in the contemporary country.

The Syrian Arab Republic is known today as a country that fiercely guards its independence and its borders, yet the modern Syrian state did not exist until 1946. Up to that point, it had been a part of one empire or another for thousands of years. The term Syria then referred to a geographical area with its northern border at the foot of the Taurus Mountains in modern-day Turkey, its

Syrian president Bashar al-Assad (second from left) addresses Lebanese leaders at a March 2002 meeting in Beirut, Lebanon. Syria has dominated the affairs of its smaller neighbor for decades. The Syrian military intervened in Lebanon's civil war, which lasted 15 years; at one time there were 35,000 troops stationed there.

southern borders along the Egyptian and Arabian deserts, and its eastern border along Mesopotamia, or modern Iraq. This area enjoyed a long coastline on the eastern shore of the Mediterranean Sea. Arabs called this area *Bilad ash-Sham*, "land of the sun."

Syria did not have defined borders until 1923, when they were created by the French and the British. These foreign nations took Greater Syria and divided it into four parts. The people who lived in the area played no part in deciding who would be Syrian, who would be Lebanese, who would be Palestinian, and who would be Jordanian. They had never thought about being citizens of a country before. They were Muslims or Christians or Jews, and were members of a family and a tribe. After 1923, they had to learn how to be members of nations. Many of them have struggled with this task, but more than 80 years later, these national identities do exist, and their people now identify themselves at least to some extent as Syrian, Lebanese, Jordanian, or Palestinian.

Fifty years ago, the leaders of these nations were united in fiercely opposing the Jewish state now in their midst. Today, each state has its own separate interests to protect, its own stance to take on handling the issue of Israel. Like all Arab peoples, national independence is a goal of Syria's, but with respect to the Arab-Israeli conflicts, Syria has always aimed for a wholly unified opposition against its enemy. This insistence on unity has often placed Syria at odds with its neighbors instead of creating alliances. In the Middle East, many people have resorted to violence and terror in an attempt to resolve their conflicts. The Syrian government has used this form of terror against its own people and supported terrorist groups attacking Turkey and Israel to achieve its political aims.

The three most prominent terrorist groups with ties to Syria are Hezbollah, Hamas, and the Abu Nidal organization. Since the mid-1980s, these groups have looked to the Syrian government for refuge and financial assistance. Israel and its Western allies have little doubt that Syria has supported these organizations, although establishing proof of ties has often been a difficult task. What complicates the matter further is that some terrorist organizations with Syrian ties operate from different countries; Hezbollah, for example, is based in Lebanon. A lasting peace between Israel and its adversaries will depend in part on whether Syria will take responsibility for these organizations and force them to stop their violent attacks.

The Middle East still commands the attention of the entire world, and Syria will have a pivotal role if a lasting peace is to be established. In the past, Syria was prepared to live at war; today, the country is forced to pay more attention to its domestic crises, the most pressing of which is a growing population with shrinking natural resources. It is clear that Syria can't afford continuous warfare for much longer. While the government may remain determined to make peace on its own terms, it cannot help but to see how much that kind of determination costs.

A flock of sheep graze beneath cliffs near Mari, Syria. Much of the country is arid steppe or dry desert, and in many areas the land is more suited for grazing animals than for farming.

The Land

In ancient times, Syria's land nurtured the growth of civilization and the birth of farming. Today, managing the land is one of the country's most serious challenges. Loss of forestland, soil erosion, low water levels, and a growing desert threaten to make Syria's land unaccommodating for its growing population.

A good portion of Syria's terrain is **steppe** and expanding desert. The steppe spreads across the country's northern region, which shares a border with Turkey; the Syrian Desert lies in the southeastern region, stretching into Jordan and Iraq. Other forms of terrain in Syria include a long coastal plain running along the Mediterranean Sea, and two mountain ranges, both of which run north to south in the western part of the country.

With desert and steppe so prominent in Syria, a dry climate challenges most areas of the country. Only 28 percent of its land area is suitable for farming. **Irrigation** from Syria's two primary rivers makes agriculture possible on 3,500 square miles (9,061 square kilometers), a small portion of the country's total area of 71,508 square miles (185,180 sq km). These rivers are the Orontes in the west, which flows north into the

Norias—water-powered wheels intended to raise water for irrigation purposes—can still be seen along the Orontes River near Hama.

Syria is mountainous along the coasts and in the southern part of the country. Major water ways include the Euphrates, Khabur, and Orontes rivers. Lake Al-Asad was created when a dam was built across the Euphrates River in the 1980s and early 1990s; opened in 1993, the dam's hydroelectric plants now produce more than 70 percent of Syria's electricity. Water from Lake Al-Asad is also used to irrigate fields.

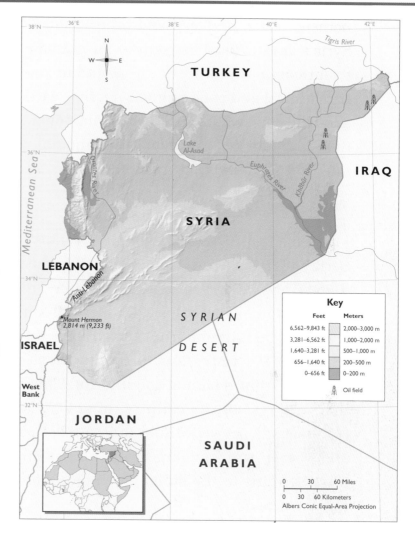

Mediterranean, and the Euphrates in the east, which flows north-west to southeast through Turkey, Syria, and Iraq.

The rest of Syria's farmland depends on rain to water crops. Some regions receive good amounts of rain in the winter, particularly along the coast and in certain parts of the mountain ranges. In those mountainous areas, the winter can be too cold to support a year-round growing season. Conversely, Syria's summers can be too hot and dry for farmland that relies on rainfall. In grassy areas of the steppe and in the mountains, the soil is often too poor to support farming. However, there is enough grass and foliage to nourish flocks of sheep and other animals. Forty-three percent of Syria's land is used as pasture for animals to graze.

Although sheep are fairly abundant in Syria, along with other agricultural and pack animals such as cattle, camels, goats, horses, and chickens, wildlife is scarce. Wild animals have been hunted and their habitats destroyed for thousands of years in Syria, at such a rate that today very few remain.

THE COASTAL REGION

Blessed with rich, red soil and a moist Mediterranean climate, Syria's short, narrow coastal strip has the most fertile farmland in the country. Along its entire 120-mile (193-km) stretch, there is no point that is more than 20 miles (32 km) wide. A chain of rocky, limestone mountains, the Nusayriyah, divides the coast from the rest of the country and prevents most of the Mediterranean's moisture from reaching the interior. This area receives more rain than the rest of the country, about 30 to 40 inches (76 to 102 centimeters) per year. Rain falls almost entirely between October and March, with the largest amount falling in January. Although it rarely rains in the summer, the humidity is very high through-out the season.

Thanks to the sea, the coastal climate is mild. It is cooler in the summer and warmer in the winter than elsewhere in Syria. The average temperature in summer is 84° Fahrenheit (29° Celsius) on the coast, compared to 90°F (32°C) and higher in the capital city, Damascus. The mild climate makes year-round farming and cultivating possible in the coastal region. Olive groves, vegetable gardens, and fruit-tree orchards are the most common commercial ventures. Citrus trees, corn, and sunflowers all grow well in this region. Hedges of cypress trees divide the fields and shield the crops from winds blowing in from the Mediterranean.

MOUNTAIN RANGES

The Nusayriyah Mountains (Jabal an-Nusayriyah) hug the Syrian coastline, stretching from the Turkish border in the north into Lebanon in the south. They are about 40 miles (64 km) wide, with their peaks averaging 4,000 feet (1,220 meters) above sea level. These mountains grow higher farther to the south, reaching their maximum height in Lebanon.

Once covered in trees, these mountains are no longer heavily

The Geography of Syria

Location: Middle East, bordering the Mediterranean Sea, between Lebanon and Turkey

Area: slightly larger than North Dakota
    total: 71,508 square miles (185,180 sq km)
    land: 71,062 square miles (184,050 sq km)
    water: 436 square miles (1,130 sq km)

Borders: Iraq 376 miles (605 km), Israel 47 miles (76 km), Jordan 233 miles (375 km), Lebanon 233 miles (375 km), Turkey 511 miles (822 km), coastline 120 miles (193 km)

Climate: mostly desert; hot, dry, sunny summers (June to August) and mild, rainy winters (December to February) along coast; cold weather with snow or sleet periodically in Damascus

Terrain: primarily semiarid and desert plateau; narrow coastal plain; mountains in west

Elevation extremes:
    lowest point: unnamed location near Lake Tiberias—656 feet (200 meters) below sea level
    highest point: Mount Hermon—9,232 feet (2,814 meters)

Natural hazards: dust storms, sandstorms

Source: Adapted from CIA World Factbook, 2002.

The fertile area south of Mount Hermon, known as the Golan Heights, has been occupied by Israel since 1967.

wooded. The little forestland that remains in Syria is located here, with cool groves of evergreen trees gracing the lower western slopes. Moisture from the Mediterranean is trapped by the steep mountains, depositing 40 to 50 inches (101 to 127 cm) of rain on the western slopes of the mountains every year. Many of the forests have disappeared because farmers have planted orchards in the hopes of taking advantage of the area's abundant rainfall. The eastern slopes and the lands beyond them receive very little of this rain, making them suitable only for grazing.

The Nusayriyah Mountains are difficult to cross, but a valley opens up just west of the city of Homs. Roads through the Homs Gap link Homs to the city of Tripoli on the Lebanese coast. Oil pipelines also travel through the gap, bringing oil from Syria and Iraq to the coast where it can be sold to other countries. To the east of the mountains, the Orontes River flows northward from its source in the Lebanese Mountains, dumping into the Mediterranean in Turkey near the Syrian border. The Orontes Valley is bounded by the Nusayriyah range to the west and the Anti-Lebanon Mountains to the east. It is one of the most heavily populated industrial and agricultural regions in the country.

Two of Syria's largest cities, Homs and Hama, lie along the Orontes, opposite the Syrian coast on the other side of the Nusayriyah range. Damascus, the capital of Syria, lies at the foot of these mountains on a narrow strip of steppe facing the Syrian Desert. Rainfall here is sparse and unpredictable with frequent droughts. Damascus often receives as little as 7 inches (18 cm) of rain in a year. A number of underground springs water an area near Damascus known as the Ghouta oasis, where fruit orchards are abundant. Flowing into the Ghouta from the mountains is the Barada River, which has enabled Damascus to prosper since ancient times.

Syria's other major mountain range, the Anti-Lebanon Mountains, lie to the east of the Orontes River. In the south, the peaks of the Anti-Lebanon form the border between Lebanon and Syria, with Lebanon lying to the west. The highest point in Syria, Mount Hermon, is in the southern part of this range near

An oasis is a fertile area in the desert that receives water from underground springs. Settlements and cities in the desert are usually built on oases.

Syria's border with Israel. The eastern slopes of the Anti-Lebanon Mountains receive very little rain, and the barren Syrian Desert takes hold of the land south and east of the mountains, continuing all the way to the borders of Jordan and Iraq.

The area south of Mount Hermon is a fertile area known as the Golan Heights, which Israel has occupied since June 1967. Many streams from the mountains provide the area with ample water. One-third of Israel's water supply originates in the Golan. Since the 1960s, there has been an ongoing international conflict over the management of the Yarmouk River, which begins in Syria, then flows along the Syrian-Jordanian border until reaching the Jordan River in Israel. The Yarmouk is the largest tributary to the Jordan, from which Israel and Jordan draw large amounts of water. Israel has often clashed with Syria over the amount of water Syria has taken from the Yarmouk. Jordan has also been in conflict with Syria over its use of the river, most heatedly during drought periods. The region's countries have yet to reach a permanent agreement over their shared water resources.

STEPPE AND DESERT

East of the Anti-Lebanon Mountains, a narrow strip of steppe in the south widens as it stretches north. This steppe covers the entire northern area of Syria, and to the far north it meets the Taurus Mountains in Turkey. Desert covers the area to the east and south of the steppe. Most of the rain in the steppe falls in the winter. Although temperatures can plunge below freezing, winters are generally mild. The winter rains make it possible to grow wheat without irrigation. Aleppo, Syria's second-largest city, lies in the western part of this steppe region. It receives about 18 inches (45.5 cm) of rain annually. The summers here are very hot and dry. Grasses, clover, and small shrubs that grow on the steppe make it ideal grazing land for animals.

The remains of a castle rise over the desert in Syria.

The large, sparsely populated desert of Syria is very rocky with little natural wildlife or vegetation. The bit of scrub that grows there during the winter months dries up as the hot, dry summer progresses. The heat and dryness increase as one goes farther south and east. About 5 inches (12.7 cm) of rain falls on the desert annually. The region can experience extreme cold as well as heat. Typically, daytime temperatures in the summer range from 90°F to

100°F (32°C to 38°C), but people have reported temperatures as high as 120°F (49°C).

At the southwestern end of the Syrian Desert lies a range of extinct volcanoes called the Jebel Arab, formerly called the Jebel Druz. The plateau north and west of the Jebel Arab is called the Hauran. It is dotted with fertile patches of volcanic soil in between stretches of basalt, which is black rock created by lava flows. Many springs in the area provide water for agriculture, and the land produces a considerable amount of wheat. In addition to receiving water from these springs, the area annually collects about 24 inches (61 cm) of rain arriving from the coast. Many ruins dating back to the Bronze Age and earlier periods reveal that the area has been settled and cultivated since ancient times. Many ancient buildings, as well as modern structures, are composed of the basalt common to the region.

VALLEYS AND PLAINS

The Euphrates River divides the northeast corner of Syria from the rest of the country. The Euphrates flows from Turkey into the Syrian steppe in the north and continues south and east through the desert into Iraq. Dams in Turkey, Syria, and Iraq regulate the river's flow. Two tributaries, the Balikh and the Khabur, are major rivers that flow north from the Euphrates.

Hydroelectric plants on these dams have helped Turkey, Syria, and Iraq bring electricity to more areas. Until dams were built, it was difficult to divert the water of the Euphrates from its deep gorge to farmland on the higher plane surrounding it. But, in a situation similar to that in Syria, Israel, and Jordan, dams and irrigation canals in Syria draw water away from the next user downstream, Iraq. With water a scarce and precious resource in this part of the region, the use of the Euphrates has been a subject of ongoing dispute among Syria, Turkey, and Iraq.

The northeast corner of Syria beyond the Euphrates is called the Jazira Plain. Rivers in the region provide the land with a good supply of water for irrigation farming. Until recently, the sparsely populated Jazira has been mostly grassland. Sources of irrigation combined with good rainfall have raised hopes that the Jazira will become a highly productive agricultural region. The discovery of oil in the Jazira has also sparked the interest of investors from Syria and neighboring countries.

The area today known as Syria was home to some of the earliest human civilizations. In Palmyra, located in the southeastern part of the country, are the remains of a temple of Baal. This was the name given to various gods worshipped by ancient people of the Middle East before the emergence of the three monotheistic religions that would reshape the region—Judaism, Christianity, and Islam.

History

Many Westerners are familiar with some aspects of Syria's ancient history through the people, places, and events of the Bible, as many biblical events occurred in or near the region of modern-day Syria. The area's original inhabitants were nomadic tribes that followed their flocks of sheep and goats from place to place in search of food and water. These people belonged to a group known as the **Semites**. They spoke a number of related Semitic languages. A small number of Syrians today still live much as these early nomads did thousands of years ago.

Syria's location has greatly helped shape its history. As a crossroads of the ancient world, it is a link between the Mediterranean cultures of the west and the civilizations of the Far East in Persia (now called Iran), India, and China. Historians and archaeologists have long believed that humans first began to live in settled communities and farm

The Phoenicians were a tribe that lived on the Syrian coast during the first millennium B.C. They developed the oldest alphabet that has ever been discovered. The Greeks developed their alphabet through contact with the Phoenicians. The Romans took the concept from the Greeks and passed it on to those who developed the modern system of the 26-letter alphabet.

the land in Mesopotamia, an area along the Euphrates River in the modern-day country of Iraq. Remains of ancient cities found in Syria reveal that it, too, was home to some of the earliest human civilizations.

Throughout most of Syria's history, the land has been ruled by one empire or another. Family and tribal ties have always been more important than government allegiance to people in this area of the world. A local tribal chief was often a more powerful figure to the local people than a distant emperor, though when an empire was at the height of its power, citizens were more likely to enjoy more stability, as they lived in organized settlements and cultivated the land with few hindrances.

Syria's great trade location was its greatest attraction to the ruling empires. One of the main routes between the Far East and the Mediterranean Sea was along overland **caravan** trails. Goods from China and India were carried to the Mediterranean coast on pack animals that had to cross the Syrian Desert. Cities along the trade routes, such as Latakia, Damascus, and Palmyra, eventually became major trading centers.

The first empires to conquer Syria came from Mesopotamia in the east. The Macedonian conqueror Alexander the Great became the first European to rule over Syria, in the fourth century B.C. Syria and the Middle East were greatly influenced by Greek culture during the centuries after Alexander's conquests. The Roman general Pompey invaded and conquered the area in 64 B.C., and Syria became a province of Rome. During this time the Roman Empire was enjoying a period of expansion and great wealth, and it benefited greatly from the caravans that passed through the major Syrian trade centers.

The Roman era was a time of religious as well as economic change. Christianity was born under Roman rule in the Jewish communities of Jerusalem and Galilee. Antioch and Damascus were important centers of early Christianity. A Jewish leader named Saul had a miraculous encounter with Jesus Christ while traveling to Damascus. After converting to the Christian faith and taking the new name of Paul, he preached Christianity while traveling through Syria and the neighboring regions of the Middle East

The Roman emperor Constantine (ca. A.D. 274–337) ended Roman persecution of the Christian church, and eventually became the first Christian emperor. He also moved the capital of the Roman Empire east, to modern-day Turkey, where he spent seven years building a glorious city, Constantinople.

and southern Europe. Paul also wrote many epistles, which later became part of the biblical New Testament.

From the cities of Palestine, the religion eventually spread across the entire Roman Empire. The Roman emperor Constantine converted to Christianity in the fourth century A.D. In A.D. 330 he moved the capital of the empire from Rome to the Greek city of Byzantium in modern-day Turkey. While Constantinople (as it was renamed) established itself as the new capital, Christianity became the state religion in Syria and the other Roman provinces. In the early fifth century, the western Roman Empire collapsed but the eastern part of the empire survived as the Byzantine Empire. For over two more centuries, Syria remained a vital center of Christianity, and a great deal of Greek and Roman culture and learning was preserved in Syrian monasteries.

Schisms eventually developed among Christians in this region. A sect called the Monophysites, established in the fifth century, proclaimed the wholly divine nature of Jesus Christ. At the Council of Chalcedon in 451, church leaders formulated an orthodox doctrine that argued for the dual nature of Christ as both human and divine being. The Monophysites, most prominent in Egypt, Syria, and Armenia, rejected the orthodox beliefs endorsed by the Council of Chalcedon. Thus developed a number of alternative sects whose descendants in present-day Syria are the Armenian Orthodox and Syrian Orthodox churches. The split that was led by the Monophysites left the Christian forces more vulnerable to foreign threats, as the Muslim conquests later demonstrated.

THE BIRTH OF ISLAM AND THE MUSLIM CONQUEST

Around 570, a man named Muhammad was born in Mecca, a town of merchants situated on a caravan route in the Arabian Peninsula. In a very short time, Muhammad would found another religion that would change the Middle East forever.

Muhammad is considered the last of the prophets by his followers, who are called Muslims. The religion Muhammad founded is known as Islam, and he was its spiritual, political, and military leader. Islam soon spread across the entire Arabian Peninsula. Arab Muslims moved quickly to conquer other people and spread their new religion. As the Arabs moved north into Syria, the Byzantines could not withstand them. The Arabs captured Damascus in 635, only a few years after the death of Muhammad. Because the region's Christians were suffering a lack of unity, the Muslim occupation met with little resistance, and much of Syria's population converted to Islam during the next few centuries.

Nonetheless, Christianity had a stronger foundation in Syria than in other Muslim-dominated territories, and some sects survived the conquest in small numbers. Their staying power owed much to the Judeo-Christian tradition's affinity with Islam and its **monotheism**. Syria thus enjoyed a moderate level of coexistence between the Christians and the Muslim authorities. However, Christians were prohibited from spreading their faith, and since then have remained the religious minority in Syria.

After Muhammad died, his followers chose a successor and gave him the title of **caliph**. The caliph took Muhammad's place as the religious and political leader of all Muslims. Thirty years after Muhammad's death, a serious disagreement over the leadership of Islam developed in the Muslim community. One group, who came to be known as **Sunnis**, supported the caliph chosen by the Muslim leaders. Others, who came to be known as **Shiites**, believed that the leaders of Islam should follow the bloodline stemming from Muhammad's cousin and son-in-law, Ali. These particular leaders are called **imams**.

The Sunni caliph founded the Omayyad dynasty, which ruled from Damascus for about 90 years. Arab Islamic rule spread across North Africa and Spain to the west and as far as western India to

Victorious knights celebrate their conquest of Jerusalem in 1099, with dead or dying Muslims and Jews pictured in the foreground. The Crusades were a series of wars fought between 1096 and 1291, during which European Christians attempted to gain control of sites they considered holy in Palestine and Syria.

the east under the Omayyads. The Omayyads were overthrown in 750 and a new caliphate, the Abbasid, established itself at Baghdad in Iraq.

Islamic culture soared to new heights during this time, while Europe, recovering from the fall of the Roman Empire, experienced a great decline. The Muslims' achievements in medicine, science, and mathematics surpassed most achievements of past cultures. Unlike the ancient Greek scientists, whose ideas were mainly theoretical, the Muslims relied on hands-on experimentation and observation. Algebra was invented under Muslim rule, and a vaccine for smallpox was developed long before it was discovered in the West.

In the 10th century, warlike Turks converted to Islam in great numbers, though they continued speaking their native language, Turkish, instead of switching to Arabic like other converts had done. They began to migrate westward, and in 1055, a group of invaders captured Baghdad. The leader of the Turks, Tughril Beg, assumed the title of sultan, but allowed the serving caliph to remain as spiritual leader.

European Christians grew concerned as the Muslim Turks moved closer to Constantinople. Across Europe and the Middle East, European kings launched a series of battle campaigns called the Crusades. On the European fronts, the kings sought to clean out the areas plagued by marauders and bandits. In the Middle East, they wanted to wrest Palestine from Muslim control as well as take over Constantinople. The Crusaders succeeded in capturing Jerusalem in 1099 and the Syrian coast in the following years. They built castles and fortresses in Syria's western mountains to defend their holdings. The brutality of the Crusaders toward their enemies convinced many Syrian Christians to convert to Islam.

During the late Middle Ages, Europe began to emerge from the ignorance that had long enveloped it. Culture and thought began to flourish again as the achievements of the Greeks and the Romans were rediscovered. Sailors from Portugal, taking advantage of advances in sailing and navigation, explored the world and discovered alternative ocean routes to India. These routes were faster, cheaper, and less cumbersome than the old caravan trails passing through the Middle East. In the centuries ahead, developments in technology, trade, and military warfare enabled European powers to continually gain greater control over the affairs of the Middle East.

OTTOMAN AND EUROPEAN RULE

During the 14th century, the Ottoman Turks came to power in Anatolia, north of Syria. In 1453 the Turks captured Constantinople from the Byzantines, a feat that stunned and delighted the Muslim world. Once the Ottomans established Constantinople (renamed Istanbul) as their capital, they began to conquer Arab lands to the south. They captured Syria in 1516.

By the 16th century, the Ottoman Empire extended across North Africa, east to Iran, into the Arabian Peninsula, down both shores of the Red Sea, north to all the areas surrounding the Black Sea, and west into Europe's Balkan Peninsula. Syria was ruled from Constantinople and became a backwater, isolated from the capital and receiving little of the central government's attention.

As devout Muslims, the Ottomans were deeply committed to putting the world under Islamic rule. Under Sultan Suleyman the Magnificent, they turned their attention to the west. When his troops attacked Vienna in 1529, it looked as though Suleyman was on the brink of capturing the heart of Europe. But the Turks did not take Vienna from the Habsburgs of Austria. In 1683 the

The reign of Sultan Suleyman I between 1520 and 1566 is generally regarded as the high point of the Ottoman Empire. Suleyman (known as "the Magnificent" and "the Lawgiver") expanded the Ottoman Empire into eastern Europe, the Arabian Peninsula, and along the Mediterranean. Greater Syria had fallen under Ottoman control in 1516.

Ottoman Turks tried again to invade Europe, but were stopped once more at Vienna.

From the birth of Islam until 1683, Muslim rulers had successfully conquered nearly every land in their sights. Muslims viewed themselves as a superior civilization with a mission to spread Allah's truth throughout the world. But the tide began to turn against them, as the Ottoman Empire eventually proved to be more vulnerable than it originally thought.

> **Muslims had contact with Eastern cultures through the caravan routes crossing their lands. Until the Arabs discovered a system of numerals in India, only the simplest forms of arithmetic were possible. Today, Arabic numerals have led to the development of higher mathematics and are used worldwide.**

Even as the Ottoman Empire threatened Europe, its power was being threatened by European technology, naval power, and commerce. After centuries of conquest, the Ottomans now had to defend what they conquered. The Europeans began to recover the lands they had lost and ultimately took over the Ottomans' territory around the Black Sea and in North Africa.

The Ottomans struggled to defend themselves against the dominant European militaries, particularly the naval forces. West Europeans had learned to build large, powerful ships that could withstand the rough seas of the Atlantic Ocean. For the Europeans, owning the seas soon meant owning most of the world as they began to conquer and colonize far-flung areas. The people of the Middle East had reaped the benefits from their location as the gateway to China and India. But when Europeans began traveling to the Far East on the ocean, the desert routes continually saw less traffic, and the world's trade began to neglect the Middle East.

The sultan's government was also losing strength in relation to the governments of Europe. European countries were developing strong central governments that could draw on all their countries' resources to coordinate war and trade. In contrast, the Ottoman government was less centralized and its local governors beyond Constantinople and Anatolia were losing control of their provinces.

In most of the outlying provinces, the sultan appointed governors known as *pashas* and transferred most government power to them. The *pashas* were given land and the task of collecting taxes for the sultan in return for military service. They took on increasing powers in their local areas, including raising troops for defense and keeping order. Many subjects of the sultan had almost no contact with his government throughout their entire lives. They paid taxes but received no government protection or services. They eventually grew more defiant. During this period, the provinces also suffered from the repeated invasions of central Asians. These invasions date back to as early as 1260, when much of Damascus and Aleppo were destroyed by Mongol conquerors.

During the 18th century, the Ottomans slowly realized they were failing to compete with Europe's growing wealth and technology. They began seeking alliances with West European countries to help protect them from Austria-Hungary and Russia threatening them from the north and east. The Ottomans purchased weapons and ships from Europeans. They also began employing them to train and advise their troops, and even commissioned some to serve as officers in the Ottoman army.

As a result of accepting European assistance, the Ottomans lost much of their power and autonomy. The stage was now set for the hungry powers of Europe to eventually take over Ottoman territory. At first, countries invaded not with guns, but with money. The Ottomans waged wars with Russia and other neighbors to the east that they couldn't win alone. Once again, they could not refuse the

European offers of aid. In exchange for that aid, they were obligated to sign treaties granting European investors rights in their territories—rights that many of their own subjects didn't have. Foreigners could conduct business in Ottoman territory with few restrictions while paying lower taxes than Ottoman subjects paid. Europeans eventually owned most of the businesses and all of the banks in the empire.

During the late 19th century, Britain withdrew the support it had been giving to the Ottomans. At this point, Germany stepped in to fill the void and began offering military aid. German archaeologists began to explore the Middle East, and ground was broken for a railroad connecting Berlin to the Persian Gulf. When World War I broke out in Europe in 1914, the Ottoman government entered the war as a German ally.

By siding with the Germans, the Ottomans found themselves fighting against Great Britain, France, and Russia. Until this point, Britain and France had been trying to keep the Ottoman government strong so that it could impede the advances of Russia. By World War I, however, they believed the empire was going to collapse anyway and began plotting to take over Ottoman territories after the war. Britain and France negotiated the Sykes-Picot Agreement, which outlined a plan for dividing the Arab lands of the Middle East between them. The plan also stated that the two countries would consult with Italy and Russia about land claims they might have. The governments approved the agreement in January 1916, but they kept it secret until the new Russian communist government disclosed the plan in October of the following year.

Europe also became involved in the Middle East in hopes of settling the issue of the Jews. A number of British politicians were supporters of **Zionism**, a Jewish movement that championed the creation of a Jewish national homeland in Palestine. Though some Jews had lived in Palestine since ancient times, after A.D. 135 most

Jewish people been forced to live in scattered settlements all over Europe and Asia. They had often suffered persecution and discrimination in European countries. In the middle of the 19th century, some European Jews began moving to Palestine to escape this persecution. By World War I, they formed a sizable minority near the coast in the southern part of the Ottoman Empire's Syrian territory. In 1917, the British government issued the Balfour Declaration, a pledge of support for a national Jewish home.

In the meantime, Britain had begun to encourage the disgruntled Arabs to revolt against the Ottoman government. The British were hoping the Arabs would join the war on their side, giving them a large fighting force in the Middle East. The emir of Mecca, Sharif Hussein bin Ali, did lead a revolt against the Ottomans, although the Arab world did not unite under him as the British had anticipated.

An Arab fighting force, led by Hussein's son Faisal, joined the British. British and Arab troops captured Damascus from the Ottomans in 1918. As military governor, Faisal claimed control of much of Syria, and made preparations to establish a new state. On October 30, 1918, the Ottomans and the British signed an **armistice** agreement. It allowed the Ottomans to keep their Turkish territory, but all the Arab territory was divided between Britain and France as part of the **mandates** enacted by the **League of Nations**, an international organization that arose from the peace treaties ending World War I. In 1920, the French army occupied Damascus and turned out Faisal, who had been proclaimed king earlier that year.

Under the terms of the League of Nations mandates, Britain would control Iraq and a part of southern Syria, which was then called Transjordan; France would control northern Syria, as well as Greater Lebanon. This area centered around the Christian community on Mount Lebanon, to which the French added a good part of the seacoast. The mandates gave Britain and France the authority to manage these areas of the Middle East until the inhabitants were ready to govern themselves. The Balfour Declaration, with its support for a Jewish homeland, was written into the mandate for Palestine.

Britain decided that the Jordan River would separate Transjordan in the east and Palestine in the west. The British government aimed to set up constitutional monarchies modeled on its own government, planning after 1920 for Faisal to be king of Iraq and his brother Abdullah to be king of Transjordan. These monarchies turned out to be more authoritarian than what the British expected of a typical constitutional monarchy. Britain opted for direct control of Palestine instead of setting up a local government, and made initial plans to turn Palestine into the Jewish homeland promised by the Balfour Declaration.

Officers of the French military garrison in Damascus stand at attention. France ruled the area from 1920 until 1946; the League of Nations officially gave France control of Syria and Lebanon in 1922.

The French created a republic in Lebanon. An area of the Mediterranean coast containing the cities of Antioch and Alexandretta (now called Iskenderun) received special status because it possessed a large Turkish minority. In 1938, the French gave this land to the Turks, and it became the Hatay province.

Although there had never really been a fully realized Syrian state to divide, many people of the Greater Syrian region deeply resented what they saw as the carving up of their homeland. They were especially angry at the loss of their seacoast to Lebanon and Turkey. Equally disturbing was that the French government treated Syria

Syrian nationalist leaders salute their supporters from the balcony of a building in Damascus, March 1936. Rioting broke out in Syria after the French government banished the nationalists to the desert near Deir el-Zor. To stop the violence, the French commissioner of Syria granted amnesty to the exiled nationalists and political prisoners. In the years between the first and second World Wars, most Syrians resented the French presence in their homeland.

like a colony, rather than as a country that would one day rule itself. In the schools, French was the language used in the classrooms, and the French national anthem was sung every day. Syrians railed against these attempts to force them to become French. It was clear to them that the French policies in Syria were for the benefit of France, not the Syrian people.

Because they were so resented, the French needed the threat of force to stay in power, and so they held onto firm control of the military. They encouraged minorities to join the military, believing they would be more loyal to the French than Sunni Muslims. Throughout Syria's history, the Druze and the Alawi religious minorities had been isolated from the mainstream population; with the French military they found opportunities that they had not had before. The local French armed forces, the Troupes Speciales du Levant, were staffed with French officers and local troops. Syrian Christians, some of whom stemmed from a line of Christians left behind by the Crusades, also found favor with the French and moved up through the ranks.

In the years following the the First World War, Syrian nationalism became a growing force, especially among educated young people in Damascus. Syrian nationalists began to demand a voice in government, and protests became more common. In 1928, France allowed the formation of the Nationalist Bloc, which folded several nationalist groups into one organization. Many of the conservative landowning families, realizing they had to protect their interests in the political process, joined the alliance. The Nationalist Bloc wrote a constitution for Syria, but France only agreed to it in 1930 after eliminating the articles that made Syria an independent nation. This modified constitution created a government made up of Syrians, though the French still held the real power.

In 1939, France finalized an agreement with Turkey and ceded the Alexandretta area to Turkey, removing yet another piece of Syria's shrunken coastline. Syrians were outraged. In the uprisings that followed, France established **martial law** and dissolved Syria's parliament. Once again, Syrians had no voice in government.

WORLD WAR II AND INDEPENDENCE

In September 1939, World War II broke out in Europe. France was quickly overwhelmed and surrendered to Nazi Germany in June 1940. A new French government was set up in the city of Vichy. The Vichy government, which controlled Syria and other French colonies, collaborated with the Nazis. In London, a provisional resistance government called Free France formed under Charles de Gaulle, with plans to continue fighting the Germans and liberate France. De Gaulle petitioned for Syria's military assistance, in return for which he promised Syria's eventual independence. Syria believed that it could further its own goals by entering the war. In 1943 Vichy France still had the Troupes Speciales du Levant in place, but the Nationalist Bloc defied them by declaring the French mandate over. They also elected a parliament and a president, Shukri al-Quwatli. By 1945, Syria had formed a national army and joined Free France and the other Allies in the war.

After the end of the war, a new international organization, the United Nations, was formed to replaced the failed League of Nations. The United Nations recognized Syria's statehood in 1946, and urged the French to leave the country. The last French troops left Syria that year on April 17, a date that is celebrated as Syria's national holiday.

Under the French mandate, economic conditions in Syria had grown worse during the Great Depression and World War II. Powerful families living in the cities owned most of the land, which was farmed by uneducated peasants. These peasants made up about two-thirds of the population. They had no access to services like education, sanitation, electricity, or paved roads. Farming methods had not changed in thousands of years. Tribal sheikhs held most of the local power in many areas.

At the same time, educated Syrians had become increasingly active in politics. Many ideas had begun to circulate as Syrians chafed under French rule. Some people wanted Greater Syria to be united under one independent government. Others believed that all Arabs had to unite for there to be a strong opposition against the Western governments that wanted to control them. They argued that Arab disunity and tribal loyalties had weakened Arabs in the eyes of Western nations. This argument was the foundation of the **Pan-Arabism** (*qawmiya*) movement. Opposing the Pan-Arabists were groups like the Muslim Brotherhood, who wanted a religious state ruled by Islamic law, similar to the way the Ottoman Empire had operated.

At the end of World War II, the Pan-Arabism movement produced official political parties in Syria, the most prominent of which was the Baath Party. *Baath* means "rebirth" in Arabic, and the Baath Party wanted a rebirth of Arab pride and the influence that Arab civilization had once enjoyed. It organized as a political party in 1947; today there are branches of the Baath Party in several Arab countries. In addition to aiming for Arab pride and unity, the Baath wanted to change the way society was organized. They supported socialism, a system in which the government, rather than private individuals, owns most of a country's industry. A socialist system— if working properly—excludes the possibility that a small group of people will own all of the country's wealth. Baath leaders felt the current system, which was managed by landowning nobility, was unfair, and they wanted to raise the standard of living of Syrian peasants.

Syria joined the Arab League in 1945. The other members were Egypt, Iraq, Lebanon, Saudi Arabia, Yemen, and Transjordan.

More states joined as they achieved independence soon after the war. Transjordan became an independent state, renamed Jordan, in 1946. The Arab League wanted to present a united face to the outside world. The member states realized that because so many of their borders had been determined arbitrarily by foreign governments, territorial disputes could escalate into wars. They agreed that differences among the Arab states should be settled by negotiation, not by war.

Hundreds of years of Ottoman rule followed by French rule left the Syrians ill-prepared to create a stable government. Following World War II, as resistance against French rule became a common goal, Syrians experienced a rare moment of unity. Once they achieved that goal, however, their unity broke down. They struggled to find something to take the place of the foreign governments.

The first 20 years of Syria's independence were marked by a series of short-lived governments and political chaos. Most of Syria's leaders during this period rose through the military and seized power by force. Syria's first government, established during the French mandate, was dominated by the landowning nobility, who consisted of pro-hierarchical, anti-reformist Sunni Muslims. It had little support among the majority of Syrians.

THE POST-INDEPENDENCE YEARS

The issue of the Balfour Declaration and the Jewish national homeland was still hanging in the air after the end of World War II. Nazi Germany had tried to eliminate the Jewish people. When the world discovered the extent of the Nazis' cruelty, many people grew more sympathetic to the Zionist cause. They supported the idea of a Jewish state.

The year after Syria became independent, Great Britain announced that it would give up its mandate in Palestine. The United Nations developed a plan to divide the territory—the

Palestine Partition Resolution. It stipulated that Palestine would be divided into two states, one Jewish and one Arab. The city of Jerusalem, which was important to both groups, would be placed under international control. The Jewish leadership in Palestine

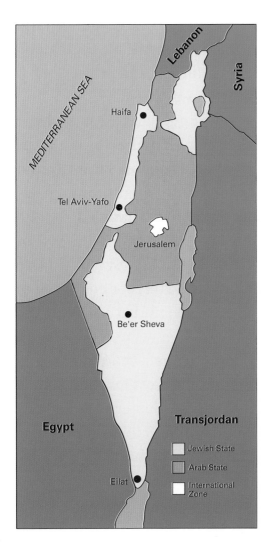
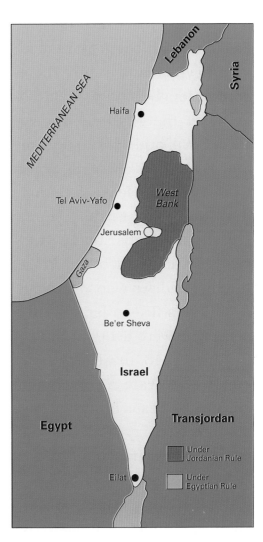

The map on the left shows the Jewish and Arab states that would have been created by the United Nations' 1947 partition plan for Palestine—a plan opposed by Syria and other Arab countries. When the British withdrew from Palestine in May 1948, the Arab forces attacked, determined to drive the Jews out of the country. The map on the right shows the boundaries of Israel at the end of the 1948–49 War of Independence.

accepted the UN resolution. In May 1948 Jewish leaders announced the independence of the new Jewish state, Israel.

The Arab League rejected the Partition Resolution. Before the resolution was officially declared, Palestinian Arabs rushed to arms to fight the Jewish state. The surrounding Arab countries quickly jumped to their aid. Many outraged Syrians still believed that Palestine was part of Greater Syria, and fought in Palestine along with Egyptians to secure the sections of land allotted to the Arabs. Jordan fought in Jerusalem for its own land interests.

When the 1948–49 war was over, the Egyptians occupied the Gaza Strip, and Jordan occupied the West Bank of the Jordan River and East Jerusalem. Syria occupied small strips of land around Lake Tiberias. However, Israel had expanded its control into areas that, according to the UN resolution, had been intended for the Palestinian Arabs. Many Palestinians fled their homes to live in refugee camps in other Arab countries, including Syria. A large number of Jews whose families had lived peacefully for centuries in Arab lands fled to Israel. These immigrants included many of the Jews who were living in Syria.

Since 1948, most Arabs have viewed Israel as a state arbitrarily created by Western governments. They have always felt that Israeli culture is Western and European, not Middle Eastern. Israel has also received a great deal of economic and military aid from Western countries, particularly the United States, throughout its history. Before the creation of Israel, the Arabs were already angry about European interference while they were under the rule of the Ottoman Empire and the mandates of the League of Nations. The Arab people's resentment of Israel thus goes hand in hand with their resentment of Western nations and their foreign policies.

In 1949, General Husni az-Zaim forced Syria's weak government out of office with backing from his troops. One *coup* followed another as Syria's military-controlled government continually changed hands. In 1954, a final coup ended the military governments, and the constitution was restored with an elected president and parliament. When parties were welcomed back into the political process, the Communist Party and the Baath Party were the best organized of the surviving parties. The Baath Party won a majority of the seats in Parliament.

The Baath Party believed the country's system of land ownership was holding back Syrian society. In 1958, in a move to break up the power of Syrian landowning families, the government limited the amount of land individuals could own. People with large landholdings were ordered to sell them within a certain time or the government would take the excess land. The government then loaned money to peasants and sold them land at very low prices. Additional land reform laws were passed in 1963 and 1980.

Syrian president Shukri al-Quwatli holds hands with Egyptian president Gamal Abdel Nasser as a sign of solidarity during Nasser's visit to Damascus in March 1958. During that year Syria and Egypt united in the United Arab Republic, but this entity lasted only until 1961, when Syria withdrew.

UNITED ARAB REPUBLIC AND THE BAATH PARTY

The president of Egypt, Gamal Abdel Nasser, was the strongest leader in the Arab world during the 1950s. Syria had been weak and unstable for several years. And so, with the Communist Party continually threatening to disrupt their political agenda, Baath leaders looked to Nasser and Egypt for assistance. They believed that uniting Syria with Egypt would provide the country with strong leadership and stability. Because Nasser was firmly against a multiple-party system, a union meant the end of the Baath Party. However, in reward for their loyalty to Nasser, Baath leaders envisioned special roles for themselves in the new state. Egypt felt that the union would stifle the threat of communism, and with Syria as an ally, it believed the two countries could more effectively fight their common enemy, Israel. The Baath politicians passed a bill through the assembly to create the United Arab Republic.

The Syrians quickly grew unhappy with an Egyptian leadership that cared more about Egypt than Syria. Syria seceded from the United Arab Republic in 1961. The new

In November 1970 Hafiz al-Assad (1928–2000) led a coup that overthrew Salah Jadid; he became president of Syria in March 1971.

government of Syria was conservative and dominated by notables, a social class of nobles with roots that reached as far back as the Ottoman Empire. Syrian government was more chaotic than ever after the breakup of the union with Egypt.

In March 1963 a small, secretive group of military officers overthrew the government. The group was dominated by members of Baath, many of whom were also members of religious minority groups. The military leaders of the alliance set up a civilian government with puppet leaders while pulling all the strings in the background. They continued to act secretly, and the public remained in the dark about who was in charge.

The Syrian political arena remained chaotic through the mid-1960s, with a rebellion erupting in Hama. The city was a center for the Sunni notable class and other religious conservatives, but the radical Muslim Brotherhood was also very active there. Conservatives feared the radical new government, and unrest grew in the city. The government put down the uprising in Hama with military force in 1964.

The fears of the notable class were realized on a larger scale when the Syrian government nationalized many private businesses in early 1965. Since then, the government has owned all businesses that distribute electricity and oil, process cotton, and conduct trade with other countries. The Baath Party was determined to break the power of the upper class and raise the conditions of the lower classes.

The 1960s saw the rise of two leaders, Salah al-Jadid and Hafiz al-Assad. These Baath Party members were also Alawis, who as a religious minority had been repressed and exploited until this point. But after successfully launching a coup in 1966, the two men helped further legitimize the Alawis in the eyes of Syrians. After the coup, Nureddin al-Atasi became prime minister, but Jadid remained the behind-the-scenes leader of Syria. Jadid had strong socialist leanings, and could not impose socialism on the country fast enough. People who came from the middle or notable class experienced discrimination in the military and the government. Meanwhile, members of the peasant class received preferential treatment and were promoted to higher ranks. Jadid established close ties with the Soviet government, which had already been providing military aid to Syria since the 1950s. It now offered economic aid as well.

THE SIX-DAY WAR AND ITS AFTERMATH

War broke out again with Israel in June 1967, after years of skirmishes between Syria and Israel near Lake Tiberias. The war, in which Israel fought the Syrian, Egyptian, and Jordanian armies, lasted only six days. It ended in complete success for Israel and disaster for the Arab states. Israel took the West Bank and East Jerusalem from Jordan, the Sinai Peninsula from Egypt, and the Golan Heights, including the town of Quneitra, from Syria.

That November, the United Nations Security Council adopted Resolution 242, which aimed at establishing a lasting peace in the Middle East. It called for Israeli withdrawal from territories it had gained in the Six-Day War, and that Arab states recognize Israel's right to exist as an independent nation. The resolution recognized the need to resolve the problem of the Palestinian refugees, although it offered no specific answers. After Resolution 242 was passed, the Israelis considered giving up territories, but at a summit in Khartoum, Sudan, the Arab states resolved against negotiations with Israel, and the two sides reached an impasse.

Most Arab states hoped to contain and control the Palestinian

Israeli troops advance during the battle for the Golan Heights in the October 1973 Arab-Israeli war. A Syrian tank burns by the side of the road.

resistance. Israel, after all, was a powerful neighbor that gained more Arab territory in each successive conflict. Until 1967, the Arabs gave the Palestinians almost no voice in negotiations with Israel. After 1967, a group called the Palestinian Liberation Organization (PLO), led by Yasir Arafat, worked more closely toward attaining a Palestinian voice in the region's affairs.

The PLO was originally based in Gaza in 1964, with links to Cairo, Egypt. In 1968, the headquarters found another temporary location in Amman, Jordan. In September 1970, the Popular Front for the Liberation of Palestine hijacked three planes, two of which were brought down to Jordanian airstrips where the passengers were held hostage. Radical Palestinians wanted to bring down the Hashemite monarchy and use Jordan as a base to attack Israel. A civil war broke out that lasted several months. One year later,

September 1971, the Jordanian army attacked remaining Palestinian militias. Hafiz al-Assad, by that time the Syrian Minister of Defense, sent an armored division into Jordan to back up the PLO, which Syria regarded as an ally against Israel. The Palestinians viewed Syria's attempt to help them as half-hearted and became angry. Meanwhile, the Jordanians felt completely alienated. They appealed to Israel and the United States for help against the Palestinians and the Syrians.

That same year, Assad took power from Jadid in a bloodless coup. Jadid controlled the Baath Party, but Assad completely controlled the military, and this had been a common route to power in Syria during the previous 25 years. Assad ordered the military to arrest Jadid and the key members of his government, and then quietly stepped into power. Jadid was imprisoned, and most of his supporters were exiled overseas. The military branch of the government was more moderate than the radical Baath Party. Immediately after the coup, Assad instituted changes to stabilize the government and shore up his power.

When national elections were held in 1971, the Baath Party nominated Assad for president, and the voters confirmed this choice in a national referendum. A referendum is an election in which the voters' only choice is whether to vote yes or no on a question, but in the case of an authoritarian government like Assad's, the legitimacy of the final vote is questionable. A 173-member legislature called the People's Council was also elected at this time. The Baath Party held a majority of the Council's seats.

In 1973, a constitution was drafted. The new Baath government was too socialist and not religious enough for conservative Sunni Muslims, who wanted the constitution to make Islam the state religion. In order to pacify the Sunnis, the Baath changed the constitution. It required that the president of Syria be Muslim, although religious freedom was otherwise guaranteed.

In that same year, the Egyptians and Syrians attacked Israel in a joined effort to regain the territory they had lost in 1967. Though Syria could not recapture the Golan Heights, Israel did return Quneitra to Syria as part of the cease-fire agreement in 1974. Before pulling out of Quneitra, however, the Israelis inflicted a great deal of damage to the town, infuriating many Syrians.

Syria was less isolated from other countries under the Assad government than it had been in the past, but it continued to steer an independent course. Syria maintained close ties with the Soviet Union, which provided military and economic assistance. This placed it in opposition to the United States.

Decades of constant political upheaval persuaded Assad to develop a more authoritarian regime. He won a firm grip on the government through control of the military, as well as independent security and intelligence units. These secret units kept a watchful eye on Syrian society and worked to prevent any political activity from taking place outside government channels. They arrested and imprisoned people they suspected of acts that were disloyal to the government.

CIVIL WAR IN LEBANON

After the PLO was banished from Jordan in 1971, Arafat moved the organization's headquarters to Lebanon. The PLO used the country as a base for attacks on Israel, which provoked Israel to retaliate. Although Lebanon had been a fairly stable country in the region, there were tensions between the Christians and Muslims who lived there. The Palestinian presence aggravated these tensions, and civil war broke out in 1975. After diplomatic negotiations failed to create peace, Syria sent troops into Lebanon.

In June 1982, Israel invaded Lebanon to support the Christian Maronites contending with the PLO. The Israelis hoped that through their support of the Maronites they could find an Arab

The remains of a U.S. Marine barracks in Beirut, Lebanon. The building was destroyed in an explosion in October 1983, and 241 Marines were killed. U.S. troops had been deployed in Beirut as part of a multinational peacekeeping force in the summer of 1982; their mission was to try to stabilize war-torn Lebanon. After similar attacks on the barracks for French and Italian troops, the peacekeeping mission ended in failure the next year.

Christian ally to fight against the Arab Muslims of the region. Israel soon occupied Lebanon, and its intervention eventually gave rise to Hezbollah, a radical Shiite Muslim group that opposed the Israeli presence there. Hezbollah used kidnappings and other terrorist tactics to further its agenda against Israel and the West.

The United Nations sent peacekeeping forces to Lebanon in 1983. A terrorist bomb killed 50 people at the American ***embassy*** in April. Another 260 U.S. Marines and 60 French soldiers died when truck bombs were detonated near their barracks later in the year. The peacekeeping countries withdrew in 1984, and a year later Israeli troops withdrew to southern Lebanon, near the Israeli border. There they continued to occupy a "security zone," from which they fought Hezbollah and tried to prevent terrorist attacks on Israeli territory. Approximately 30,000 Syrian troops remained stationed in Lebanon as well.

Assad continued to endorse the Baath opinion that Arabs are stronger working together than they are working separately. As a result, he consistently opposed negotiations and treaties between Israel and individual Arab states. He wanted the Arab states to negotiate from a position of unity and strength. He also insisted that Israel had to uphold its end of Resolution 242 and withdraw to its old borders before the Arabs would agree to a lasting peace. The Syrian leadership believed the Arab world suffered a blow in 1979 when Anwar el-Sadat, the president of Egypt, signed a separate peace treaty with Israel. Egypt recognized Israel and established ***diplomatic relations*** with it in exchange for Israel's return of the Sinai Peninsula to Egypt.

The Western world hailed the treaty, which was mediated by the United States, as a giant step toward establishing peace in the Middle East. But many Arabs were enraged, feeling their strongest ally had betrayed them. They ejected Egypt from the Arab League and moved the League's headquarters from Cairo, Egypt, to Tunis, Tunisia. Egypt's membership in the Arab League would not be restored until 1989, when League headquarters were moved back to Cairo. In 1981 Sadat was assassinated by extremists who were opposed to Egypt's peaceful negotiations with Israel.

The 1980s was a difficult decade for Syria. Several years of drought debilitated its agriculture, and the troops stationed in Lebanon were a drain on the Syrian economy. Syria sided with Iran against Iraq when war erupted between the two countries in 1980, but it did not fight in the conflict. The decision to support Iran over another Arab state isolated Syria from its allies. In addition to all of these problems, unrest in the country prompted the government to take harsh measures against its own people.

The Muslim Brotherhood continued to oppose Baath Party rule and to clamor for a conservative Sunni Muslim state. In 1979, the Muslim Brotherhood initiated a series of attacks targeting Baath Party officials and members of the military. In response to these attacks, the government cracked down harshly on the Muslim opposition. Membership in the Muslim Brotherhood became a crime punishable by death. In 1982, an elite military unit led by Assad's brother Rifaat attacked and bombed the city of Hama, rooting out cells of the Muslim Brotherhood that were sheltered there. Although the exact figures are not known, as many as 25,000 people died in the attacks.

During the 1980s, Syria angered Western nations by supporting the activities of Hezbollah and other terrorist organizations in Lebanon. Syria was known to supply these organizations with weapons, funding, and military training. In addition, several terror-ist attacks overseas were traced back to Syria, including an attempt to plant a bomb aboard an Israeli jetliner traveling from London to Tel Aviv, Israel.

After more than 10 years of continuous fighting in Lebanon, the Lebanese parliament, aided by Syria and other Arab countries, created an agreement for peace and strong civil government at a 1989 meeting in Saudi Arabia. The agreement, called the Taif Accord, outlined plans for a government in which power would be shared more fairly between Christians and Muslims. It also called for the complete withdrawal of Israeli troops from Lebanon.

The agreement stated that Syrian troops would withdraw from Beirut and retreat to Lebanon's Bekaa Valley once Israeli troops were gone, and that the troops would completely withdraw from Lebanon in two years. Also, Syria and Lebanon would decide together whether to continue using Syrian troops in Lebanon. Israel did not withdraw its troops from Lebanon, instead staying on to fight the Hezbollah in the south until May 2000. One year later, Syrian troops made initial efforts to pull out of the region.

The Syrian economy improved in the 1990s thanks to increased oil prices and good harvests. The government also made slight changes to relax government control of the economy. To sustain its economy, however, Syria continued to rely heavily on foreign aid from countries of the Persian Gulf, as well as those of the West. For years, Syria owed billions of dollars to the Soviet Union.

THE PERSIAN GULF WAR

Iraqi president Sadaam Hussein invaded the tiny Arab country of Kuwait in 1990. He soon annexed Kuwait, claiming it as part of Iraq. King Fahd of Saudi Arabia, who feared his own country might be Iraq's next target, asked for international support against Saddam Hussein. When diplomacy failed, a coalition of 34 countries, led by the United States, went to war with Iraq. Although some states of the Arab League chose not to go to war against another Arab country, Syria and many other Arab countries fought against Iraq.

After the Persian Gulf War, Syria's relations with the international community were a bit more open. When the United States and the Soviet Union invited the Middle Eastern countries to a peace conference in Madrid in 1991, Syria attended. At this conference, the Arab countries expressed a willingness to make peace, acknowledge Israel's right to exist, and establish diplomatic relations. In return for peace, they insisted that Israel turn Palestinian-occupied territory over to the Palestinians so they could establish their own state. They also demanded that Palestinian refugees living in other countries be allowed to return to their former homeland.

Throughout the 1990s, Syria participated in peace negotiations with Israel several times, but there were few advances. The Syrian government continued to insist there would be no peace until all Arab peoples, including the Palestinians, are at peace with Israel. In 1994, Jordan disrupted Syria's agenda by becoming the second Arab country to sign a peace treaty with Israel.

Israel has claimed a willingness to return the Golan Heights in exchange for peace and normal relations with Syria, but the two sides cannot agree on their borders. Syria insists on restoring the line defined in the 1949 armistice. Israel wants the border that had been established by the League of Nations mandates in 1923. The difference is only a few miles, but the 1949 armistice line gives Syria access to Lake Tiberias, a valuable water resource, and the 1923 international border does not.

A Syrian woman faints after mourning in frenzy after the death of Hafiz al-Assad, who ruled Syria for nearly three decades.

The Israelis and the Palestinians also began negotiating ways to live together peacefully during the 1990s. With the Oslo Accords, signed in Norway in 1993, each side recognized the other's political and civil rights in Palestine. Israel also recognized the Palestinian Authority, made up of PLO leaders, as representative of the Palestinian people and agreed to negotiate with Yasir Arafat. In return, Arafat renounced the use of "terrorism and other acts of violence," which until the Oslo Accords had been the most common fighting tactic of the Palestinians. Israel agreed to allow the Palestinians' limited self-rule in the West Bank and the Gaza Strip as well. To carry out their self-rule, the Palestinians elected Yasir Arafat as president of the Palestinian National Authority in 1996.

Although the PLO had renounced terrorism, several other terrorist organizations remained active in Israel, including Hezbollah and Hamas. The Israeli people were sharply divided in their opinions about peace with the Palestinians. As a result, they elected several different leaders during this time, all with different attitudes toward peace. Negotiations broke down, and violence erupted again between the Israelis and the Palestinians in 2000.

Negotiations between Syria and Israel also stalled during that year, as neither side would give up any of its demands. In May, Israel finally pulled its troops out of southern Lebanon. In 2001, the Arab League asked its members to break off all relations and all negotiations with Israel as long as it continued to use violence to deal with the Palestinians.

Syrian president Hafiz al-Assad died in June 2000 after 30 years as Syria's leader. The relative stability in Syria under Assad's leadership was based on his personal power and control. Many wondered if the Syrian government would sink into chaos after his death. The government and the Baath Party moved quickly to ensure that there would be no sudden changes in Syrian politics.

Hafiz al-Assad had been preparing his son Bashar to become

president since 1994. On the day Assad died, government leaders loyal to him named Bashar commander-in-chief of the armed forces. Firm control of the military would eliminate the possibility of a military coup. Bashar al-Assad took his father's place as Secretary-General of the Baath Party that same day. The Syrian constitution required that the president be at least 40 years old, and Bashar was only 34. The constitution was quickly changed, and the Baath Party nominated Bashar al-Assad for president. He was elected in a national referendum that July.

Bashar's followers believe he is more politically liberal than his father was. They often cite Bashar's effective management of a domestic anti-corruption investigation that took place before his instatement as president. Nonetheless, since he took office there have been no major changes in Syrian politics. He has released some political prisoners, but others have been convicted and imprisoned for speaking out

Bashar al-Assad became president of Syria after his father's death in 2000. Until 1994, Bashar had been a medical doctor practicing ophthalmology in London; however, in that year Bashar's brother Basil died and Hafiz al-Assad, who had planned for Basil to take his place, quickly called Bashar home.

against the government. He has discussed establishing a Syrian stock exchange and legalizing private banks. However, his power depends on the continued loyalty of his father's supporters. He cannot afford to alienate them with policy changes that stray too far from their socialist beliefs.

In June 2001, Syria withdrew most of its troops stationed in Beirut and relocated them elsewhere in Lebanon, in accordance with the first step outlined in the Taif Accord. The Syrian troops were moved to the Bekaa Valley near the Syrian border the following April, but it is unlikely that those troops will move farther back in the near future.

Syria has continued trying to take a larger role in the world community at the beginning of the 21st century. In October 2001, Syria was elected to a temporary seat on the UN Security Council, replacing Tunisia. That same month, Syria applied for membership in the World Trade Organization, an international body managing the regulations of trade between different countries.

At a March 2002 meeting of Arab League nations in Beirut, Crown Prince Abdullah of Saudi Arabia presented a plan for peace between the Arab states and Israel. After some debate and modifications, the Arab League adopted the plan. It states that fighting will never resolve the differences between Israel and the Palestinians. Instead, it calls for Israel to return all land taken in the Six-Day War, to allow for the return of Palestinian refugees to Israel, and to agree to a Palestinian state in the West Bank and the Gaza Strip with its capital in East Jerusalem. In return, it calls on all Arab states to make peace and establish "normal relations" with Israel. President Bashar al-Assad was present at this meeting and endorsed the plan.

A mosque with four minarets in Aleppo, one of the oldest cities in the world. It is believed that Abraham (Ibrahim), an ancient figure revered today by Jews, Christians, and Muslims alike, once stopped near the site of this city in northern Syria.

The Economy, Politics, and Religion

Syria has a socialist economy. The government owns and controls many industries and sets prices for essential items, especially staple foods like grain. All Syrian banks are government owned. Every five years, the president draws up an economic plan dictating economic goals and priorities for the next five years. In controlling the economy, the government has tried to equalize the incomes and opportunities available to people from different social classes and in different areas of the country.

In recent years, the Syrian government has tried to attract more private investment in the Syrian economy, with limited success. The government still regulates the Syrian economy very closely. In order to attract foreign investors—who in the past have been dissuaded by Syrian's state-run economy—laws have been passed in recent years to improve terms for foreign investors, simplify currency exchange rates, and pave the way for foreign banks to do business in the country.

The government owns utilities like electrical power generation, telephone lines, and water distribution. The government also owns the railroads, trucks, and buses that move products from one area of the country to another. Heavy industry, which includes oil drilling and mining, is also government owned. Private individuals and businesses are allowed to own farms and factories, as well as shops and other small businesses. The government also allows joint public and private ownership of certain types of businesses in order to encourage the investment of private money without the complete loss of government control. The government owns about 25 percent of these joint-venture firms.

Only one in four Syrians participates in the workforce. Of those people who are employed, quite a few are forced to have more than one job to supplement their incomes. One reason for this low level of employment is the

A Syrian Railways tank locomotive chugs to a stop in a depot yard at Sergayah, an oasis near the border with Lebanon. Syria has a network of railways that covers 1,709 miles (2,750 km), including lines linking the country to Lebanon and Iraq.

The flag of Syria, which was adopted in 1982, is very similar to the flags of several of its neighbors. Iraq's flag follows the same design but adds a third star and an Arabic inscription. Egypt's flag includes the red, white, and black horizontal stripes, but instead of the stars a heraldic eagle is centered on the flag.

Syrian population's uneven distribution. Almost half of all Syrians are school-age children. The employment levels of Syrian women are especially low. In the cities, only one woman out of every ten engages in paid employment.

Forty percent of Syria's 4.7 million workers earn their living in agriculture, 20 percent work in industry, and 40 percent work in service industries. Those in the service industries include doctors, teachers, bus drivers, and maids. The unemployment rate—the percentage of people who are available to work but don't have jobs—is 20 percent. Many Syrians have avoided unemployment by working overseas, particularly in the Gulf Arab states. The money they send home to their families is a much-needed boost to the economy, but Syria still needs a better-educated workforce in order to compete in the modern global economy.

The Syrian government owes $22 billion to foreign banks in Western Europe and in Russia, who inherited Syria's debts from the former Soviet Union. Every year, Syria receives $199 million in foreign aid, most of which comes from the oil-producing Gulf states. The European Union and Japan have also given Syria economic assistance.

A craftsman uses old methods to create bright fabric prints at a souq in Aleppo. The textile industry has traditionally employed many Syrians.

MODERNIZATION

Oil is Syria's most lucrative industry. Oil and petroleum products account for the bulk of Syria's export revenue. Unfortunately, Syria appears to lack the vast oil reserves that bless many other Arab states. Despite Syria's poverty, high unemployment, and economic problems, modern development has improved the country's standard of living a great deal since World War II.

By 1992, 95 percent of Syria's villages had electricity. Most areas of the country also have water pipes and a safe supply of clean drinking water. Some areas, however, still rely on water that is shipped in on trucks. With 1.3 million telephone lines in use in 2003, telephones have become more common to Syria, but there are some households in rural areas that still do not own them.

Many roads have been laid to open up rural areas. In 1997, about 23 percent of Syria's roads were paved. Syria's mountains have been a serious obstacle to **exports** in the past because they cut off the interior of the country from the coast, where goods can be shipped overseas. A railroad that travels across the mountains between the agricultural region of the Ghab and the port of Latakia has allowed faster, more efficient transportation of products to the coast.

The Economy of Syria

Gross domestic product (GDP*): $17.93 billion

GDP per capita: $1,000

Inflation: 0.3%

Natural resources: petroleum, phosphates, chrome and manganese ores, asphalt, iron ore, rock salt, marble, gypsum, hydropower

Agriculture (27% of GDP): wheat, barley, cotton, lentils, chickpeas, olives, sugar beets, beef, mutton, eggs, poultry, milk (2000 est.)

Industry (23% of GDP): petroleum, textiles, food processing, beverages, tobacco, phosphate rock mining (2000 est.)

Services (50% of GDP): government services, banking, insurance, tourism, transportation (2000 est.)

Foreign trade:

    Imports—$4 billion: machinery and transport equipment, food and livestock, metal and metal products, chemicals and chemical products (2000 est.)

    Exports—$5 billion: crude oil, textiles, fruits and vegetables, raw cotton (1998 est.)

Currency exchange rate: U.S. $1 = 51.578 Syrian pounds (2003)

*GDP, or gross domestic product, is the total value of goods and services produced in a country annually.
All figures are 2001 estimates unless otherwise noted.
Sources: CIA World Factbook, 2002; bloomberg.com.

AGRICULTURE AND INDUSTRY

Syria has been forced to find better ways to feed its growing population. For this reason, the government has focused heavily on agriculture in its economic planning. Syria faces several environmental problems that impact the land's ability to feed its people. Only 20 percent of Syria's farmland is watered by irrigation. The rest is dependent on unreliable rains and is frequently hit by droughts. In addition, too many wells have depleted the ground water, and many of the rivers are becoming polluted. Syria's soil also needs serious attention. Topsoil erosion, plus the repeated growth of the same crops on the same fields without the addition of fertilizer, has exhausted the soil in many areas. Fertilizers and crop rotation are necessary to improve the soil's nutrient content so healthy crops can grow.

Syrians have been making and exporting textiles for hundreds of years. Cotton is one of Syria's principal crops. Cotton cloth and cotton clothing are manufactured in Syria. Silk weaving and leather tanning are also important industries. In addition to textiles, Syrian factories produce soap, cement, glass, matches, bottled beverages, fertilizer, processed foods, and household appliances.

Over time the private business sector has been gradually expanding. Shops have always been privately owned. Merchants and artisans often work in family-owned businesses. Many Syrian products are still made by hand in small artisans' workshops, just as they have been for centuries.

POLITICS

Syria is a republic whose military dominates government and political life. The Syrian constitution took effect on March 13, 1973. The constitution invests almost all the government's power in the president, who is also the commander-in-chief of the armed forces and Secretary-General of the Baath Party. The constitution is designed to ensure that the president and the Baath Party will remain in power. The president has control of almost all government appointments, foreign relations, the armed services, and the economy. He has the power to declare war, draft all the country's laws, and make changes to the constitution.

President Bashar al-Assad is a member of the Alawi religious minority. Although they form a small percentage of the Syrian population, Alawis and other minorities dominate the military and hold many prominent government and Baath Party positions.

The president is elected to a seven-year term in a national popular referendum. All Syrians over the age of 18 are eligible to vote. The Baath Party nominates one candidate to the presidency. The people then vote whether or not to approve the party's nominee. Syrian presidential elections do not involve a choice between candidates, and in contrast to countries with democratic elections, it would be extremely rare for a Syrian presidential candidate to not win the public vote. The president appoints his vice presidents, his prime minister, several deputy prime ministers, and a council of ministers to head up the government.

Syrians elect representatives to the 250-member People's Council for four-year terms. The constitution guarantees the Baath Party 167 seats on the People's Council. Two-thirds of the seats are held by members of the National Progressive Front, a coalition of political parties dominated by the Baath. The National Progressive Front was created to prevent rival political parties from challenging the Baath. The People's Council approves or vetoes laws written by the president.

The Syrian legal system is a mixture of Islamic, French, and

Syrian and Lebanese youths participate in summer military training for initiation into a Palestinian opposition group, July 1999, near Damascus. Syria's support for organizations dedicated to the destruction of Israel led to its categorization by the U.S. government as a state that supports terrorism.

Ottoman law. There are separate religious, civil, and criminal courts. The president appoints judges in the Syrian courts to four-year terms. There are also military courts that operate apart from the judicial system.

Two and a half years of military service is mandatory for all men over 19. The Syrian military includes 400,000 active-duty and reserve troops. The president handpicks the members of elite military units. Because they depend on the president for their position, they tend to be loyal to him. Only these troops are allowed to be stationed in Damascus. This law is designed to prevent a military coup of the presidency.

The president also maintains security and intelligence agencies that operate independently of one another and answer only to him. These secretive agencies monitor every aspect of Syrian life. Agents often disguise themselves as people working in the general population. The agencies are an important key to the president's tight control over the country, and further ensure that he will stay in power.

Syrian citizens basically have no real civil rights. They have no freedom of speech, and everything they say may be overheard by intelligence agents or secret police. Gatherings for anything but religious worship are very closely monitored and treated with sus-picion. The government fears grassroots political organizations that might try to undermine its power. The constitution grants Syrians certain rights, though in practice the government has withheld many of those rights. The primary reason that Syrians have lost their civil liberties is that the country has been in a state of martial law since 1963. Martial law is often used to justify bypassing the judicial system and denying citizens their civil rights.

RELIGION

The Syrian constitution provides for freedom of religion, and for the most part, the government respects it in practice. The constitu-tion does, however, require the president of Syria to be a Muslim, and also establishes that Syrian Muslims should be governed by Islamic religious law, known as **Sharia**, in addition to the civil and criminal legal codes. The Islamic legal courts collectively make up one branch of the Syrian judicial system.

Almost all Syrians are monotheists, people who believe in only one God. The majority of Syrians are Sunni Muslims. Sixteen percent of Syrians belong to minority Muslim sects, and about 10 percent are Christians. Although Syria used to have a sizable Jewish population, most Jews have emigrated in response to the tension between Syria and Israel.

The Islamic faith dominates Syrian culture and daily life as it does in most Islamic countries. *Islam* means "submission" in Arabic. Muslims are supposed to submit themselves to God (*Allah*

Muhammad and his followers fled Mecca and moved to Medina in A.D. 622. This journey is called the *Hijrah*. For Muslims, 622 is the first year of the Islamic era, which is marked by the *Hijrah* and follows the lunar instead of the Western calendar. Years of the *Hijrah* are designated with the initials A.H., which stands for anno hegirae, (year of the *Hijrah*). A.H. is used in a similar fashion to the initials B.C. and A.D.

in Arabic) and follow the teachings of Muhammad, whose sayings are recorded in the Muslim holy book, the **Qur'an** (or Koran). Islam teaches that the Qur'an is the word of God revealed to Muhammad by the angel Gabriel. In addition to the Qur'an, Muslims follow the **Sunna**, a collection of sayings and teachings of the Prophet. Together, the Qur'an and the *Sunna* make up *Sharia*, which for hundreds of years was the only form of law in several Muslim countries.

Muslims believe the words of the Jewish prophets of the biblical Old Testament. They also believe that Jesus Christ, the founder of Christianity, was a prophet sent by God. They consider Jews and Christians fellow "people of the Book." But for Muslims, Muhammad was the final prophet sent by God to correct and clarify errors made by the earlier prophets. He was the last prophet God sent because his life and testaments are the final and perfect truth.

The five pillars of Islam are actions that every faithful Muslim is supposed to perform. The first is to believe and faithfully recite the *Shahada*, the declaration of the faith, which consists of these words: "There is no god but Allah, and Muhammad is His Prophet." The second pillar is prayer. There are two types of prayer in Islam, *Salat* and *Du'a*. *Salat* is a set of prayers that Muslims must say five times each day while they face Mecca. These prayers consist of the *Shahada* and passages from the Qur'an. *Salat* is performed at sunrise, midday, afternoon, sunset, and evening. The second form of prayer, *Du'a*, is unstructured personal prayer, and is not required.

The third pillar is the **hajj**. All Muslims are required, if capable, to make a pilgrimage to Mecca at least once in their lifetimes. The hajj takes place every year between the seventh and tenth days of the last month in the Muslim calendar. Pilgrims take part in a festival at the Mosque of Mecca during the hajj. Although it is not required, many pilgrims also travel to Medina to pray at Muhammad's grave. The fourth pillar is *Sawm*, a required fast during the month of **Ramadan**, the ninth month of the Islamic calendar. The fifth pillar is *Zakat* (charity), which requires Muslims to give money to the needy.

The Muslim place of worship is called a mosque. The wall of the prayer hall that faces toward Mecca is marked by a special niche indicating the direction worshipers should face during prayer. It is common in Muslim countries to hear men called *muezzins*

An illustrated page from the Qur'an, the holy book of Islam. Syrian law is based on Islamic laws outlined in the Qur'an, the *Sunna*, and the *Hadith*, a collection of stories about the prophet Muhammad.

announce the next prayer time from the tops of minarets, or tall towers.

The Muslim day of prayer is Friday. It is a day off from work and school in Islamic countries, and many people worship at a mosque on that day. Prayers in the mosque are generally led by a prayer leader called an *imam*.

Islamic teachings forbid using force to convert non-believers. Muslims have to choose to believe. When Muslims conquered new lands, monotheists were allowed to continue practicing their own religions freely, although they had the option of converting to Islam, which had social and legal advantages. Those who weren't "people of the book" had three choices: they could convert, become slaves, or die. Technically, however, they were not forced to choose Islam.

Although Muslims are not supposed to use force in converting others, traditional Islamic law does impose on them a religious obligation to spread the Islamic faith throughout the world. This has been interpreted to mean that all the people of the world should become either Muslims or subjects of Muslim rulers. This concept of spreading Islamic law is known as jihad. It is usually interpreted as waging a holy war. Muhammad and his followers were fighting the jihad when they conquered the Middle East. Those who die fighting the jihad are considered martyrs for the faith. The Qur'an states that those who fight the jihad will be rewarded on earth and in heaven.

MUSLIM SECTS

All Muslims follow the Qur'an and *Sharia*. Because these two texts guide all Islamic sects, the differences among the sects are generally more rooted in society and politics than religious beliefs. Early in the history of Islam, a disagreement developed over the religious leadership of the Muslim community. Sunni Muslims believed that the leader of Islam should be elected. Shiites believed that the position should be inherited through the line of Ali, Muhammad's cousin.

Sunni means "orthodox path" and refers to people who follow the *Sunna.* Most of the Muslims throughout the world are Sunnis. Shiites form the majority in only four Arab countries: Lebanon, Bahrain, Iran, and Iraq. They often tend to be more radical in their religious practices than Sunni Muslims, although the Muslim Brotherhood, a Sunni sect, is just as radical in practice as many Shiite sects. The majority of Shiites are members of the lower social classes, living in rural areas. Most strongly believe in martyrdom, and the theme of persecution runs through the general Shiite interpretation of Islamic history. They are more flexible with Islamic doctrine, stressing that it can be modified and expanded on. Some Shiites have broken off into additional sects, such as the Imami Shiites (also knows as the Twelver Shiites) and the Ismailis.

Some Shiite sects have adopted a policy of extreme secrecy. As a result, their exact beliefs are not well known or understood. Believers can only be born into these groups, which do not accept converts. They guard their beliefs carefully for fear of being perse-cuted as heretics by the Sunni majority. Several of these sects form sizable minorities in areas of Syria.

The Alawis form the largest Muslim minority group in Syria. They have traditionally lived in western Syria in the Nusayriyah Mountains near Latakia and have had little contact with outsiders. The Alawis' situation is changing, however, as they have risen to power in Syria through the military, the government, and the Baath Party. Today more of them live in Damascus, attend school, and mix with the general population. Most Alawis believe that Muhammad, Ali, and Salman, a friend and companion of Muhammad, are divine. For this reason, Sunnis consider Alawis heretics, accusing them of denying that there is only one God. Alawi clerics have attested that the Alawis are indeed Shiite Muslims who

Pope John Paul II enters the Church of St. Paul in Damascus during his May 2001 visit to Syria. Although most Syrians are Muslims, the country does have a larger Christian population than most other Arab countries. About 10 percent of Syrians are Christian.

faithfully follow the teachings of the Qur'an.

The Ismailis are a small group of Imami Shiites. In the past, they have tended to be religious extremists and political revolutionaries. Their beliefs are shrouded in secrecy. A small number of Ismailis live in villages in the western mountains of Syria. The Druze are an offshoot sect of the Ismailis, with doctrines so unconventional that much of Islam does not consider them to be really Muslim. The Druze live in Damascus, Aleppo, and around the Jebel Arab range.

The Yazidis are a very small Kurdish-speaking minority concentrated in a few villages northwest of Aleppo. Little is known about their beliefs other than that they honor the Bible and the Qur'an.

Most of Syria's Christians live in cities. Before the Muslim conquest, almost all Syrians were Christians. Although most converted to Islam, a number of them did not. Today, Syrian Christians belong to a number of different Christian churches. These include the Syrian Orthodox Church, the Armenian Orthodox Church, the Greek Orthodox Church, the Greek Catholic Church, and the Syrian Catholic Church. Christian liturgies (rites of worship) are conducted in a number of different languages: Arabic, Greek, Armenian, Aramaic, and Syriac.

A Syrian woman helps a young girl at the entrance to a mosque in Damascus. Syria's population is more than 17 million.

The People

rabs make up the vast majority of Syria's population. Their language is Arabic. The bulk of the population has its origins in the Semitic tribes that populated the area in ancient times, but their culture is greatly influenced by the Arabs who invaded Syria in the seventh century. Syrian society is shaped by the core values of religion and family. Today, Syria's leaders aim to achieve a balance between preserving old traditions and taking steps forward in fields such as health care and education.

HEALTH CARE

Thanks to improvements in health care, people in Syria are living longer now than they used to. The ratio of doctors to people is five times greater than it was in 1963, though hospitals are still scarce outside the larger cities and towns. In an effort to ensure that all Syrians receive adequate health care, the government has established free health centers for basic services, including vaccinations and preventive care. Seventy percent of these centers are located in rural areas. Private health care is also available, and many people prefer to use it. Wider access to vaccinations and medical care has contributed to the high growth rate of Syria's population, as death rates and infant mortality have dropped while the birth rate has remained high.

EDUCATION

Literacy and education have been on the rise in Syria since World War II, though training enough teachers to educate the large number of schoolchildren in Syria has been a challenge for the educational system. In the 1940s, less than one-fourth of Syrian children attended school. Today, education is mandatory for all children between the ages of six and eleven. All Syrian school children wear green military-style uniforms and go to school every day except Friday, the Muslim day of worship.

Primary and secondary education is free in Syria. Christians often attend their own private schools, but all schools in Syria are required to teach the state curriculum. The Syrian education system has been criticized for emphasizing memorization of facts over thinking skills. Asking questions is often discouraged in school because it is seen as a challenge to authority.

Children between the ages of six and eleven attend primary school. This is followed by three years of

A small number of Syrian Christians still speak Aramaic, the language used in Syria 2,000 years ago. A Semitic language, Aramaic was the language of Syria and much of the Middle East for thousands of years before Arabic swept the country in the seventh century. It was the everyday spoken language of Jesus Christ and his disciples. Today, speakers of Aramaic still live in a few villages near Damascus.

The heaviest concentration of Syria's population can be found along the coast or around Damascus, the capital. Other populated areas include the city of Tadmur (also known as Palmyra) near the center of the country, and the area along the borders with Iraq and Turkey, particularly along the Euphrates and Khabur rivers.

secondary education, much like middle school or junior high school in the United States. Three additional years of secondary education are available to a limited number of students between the ages of 15 and 18. Students have to take an exam to qualify for those spots in the secondary schools. After completing secondary schools, if students pass their exams, they may be eligible for a university education, or receive vocational or technical training. Vocational training prepares students for careers in industry, agriculture, or primary education.

The Syrian government has set goals to increase the number of Syrians who can read and write. In addition to educating children, the government offers literacy classes for adults. More people can read and write in Syria today than ever before: 70 percent of the population is literate (those aged 15 or over who can read and write). But the number of literate adults in Syria is still much lower than it is in many parts of the world. Many families place more value on educating their sons than their daughters. City children usually receive more years of education and attend better schools than children in rural areas, though educational opportunities for rural children have improved steadily over the last 40 years.

Syria has four universities: the University of Damascus, the University of Aleppo, Tishrin University in Latakia, and Al-Baath University in Homs. All are owned and controlled by the government. University education in Syria is not free, but it is inexpensive. The government has been trying to encourage more students to study science, engineering, and agriculture.

Wealthy Syrians often choose to attend European universities. Although the percentage of Syrians holding university degrees is still small, there has

The People of Syria

Population: 17,155,814
Ethnic groups: Arab 90.3%, Kurds, Armenians, and other 9.7%
Religions: Sunni Muslim 74%; Alawite, Druze, and other Muslim sects 16%; Christian (various sects) 10%; small numbers of Jewish, located in tiny communities in Damascus, Al Qamishli, and Aleppo
Language: Arabic (official), Kurdish, Armenian, Aramaic, French, Circassian widely understood
Age structure:
    0–14 years: 39.3%
    15–64 years: 57.5%
    65 years and over: 3.2%
Population growth rate: 2.5%
Birth rate: 30.11 births/1,000 population
Death rate: 5.12 deaths/1,000 population
Infant mortality rate: 32.73 deaths/1,000 live births
Life expectancy at birth:
    total population: 69.08 years
    males: 67.9 years
    females: 70.32 years
Total fertility rate: 3.84 children born/woman
Literacy (age 15 and older): 70.8% (1997 est.)

All figures are 2002 estimates unless otherwise noted.
Source: CIA World Factbook, 2002

been a significant increase in higher education in recent years. In addition, more people from the rural areas and from the lower classes have access to higher education today than they did in the past. As a result, the educated middle class in the cities is growing.

Syrians with university educations tend to have slightly different social values from the general population. For example, they often have more liberal attitudes about the roles of men and women in society. Educated women are far more likely to work outside the home than less-educated women.

FAMILY

The idea of national loyalty is very new to the country. Syrians' loyalty is primarily to their families—and on a larger level, their confessional (religious) affiliation. All other ties—friendship, work relationships, political connections—come second. To a Syrian, the family means a vast network of relatives, not just parents and their children. For many centuries, Syrian families were organized into clans and tribes. Many Syrians, particularly Bedouins, Kurds, Alawis, and Druze, still see themselves as members of a tribe.

For this reason, family connections still strongly determine a person's place in society. The best way to achieve wealth or power is through the channels of wealthy or powerful relatives. In business and government, people prefer to hire and promote other family members. Individuals with favors to dispense will pass them on to a family member before anyone else.

Developments in the educational system are bringing slight changes to Syrian society. Values in Damascus and Aleppo tend to be less conservative than they are in rural areas. But obedience and loyalty to the family are important to some extent in every social group. Families are very involved in choosing marriage partners for those of the proper age. Among the educated middle class of Damascus and Aleppo, people usually choose their own spouses,

An unhappy bride leaves with her new husband after their arranged marriage. It is still common for families to arrange marriages for their children, particularly in the rural areas of Syria.

but they still require their families' approval before marrying. Among other groups, particularly in the rural areas, arranged marriages are still very common.

Young Syrian men and women are encouraged to marry within their families. Marriages between first cousins are considered ideal among Syrian Muslims, although most Christian groups forbid this practice. Syrians often find that marrying a person with close blood ties is easier than trying to divide their loyalties between two families. On the other hand, relatives sometimes view marriages between unrelated partners as a way to create useful ties with other families.

When a woman marries she takes on her husband's family ties

and obligations, but her own family ties remain as well. She is always permitted to return to her parents' home. Islamic law permits a man to have more than one wife as long as he can afford it. This practice is legal but very rare in modern Syria. A woman married to a Syrian citizen may not leave the country without her husband's permission.

Divorce is permitted under Islamic law. The divorce rate in Damascus is about 20 percent. Divorce is less common elsewhere in Syria. Men or their families are automatically awarded custody of sons older than nine and daughters older than eleven when a couple divorces. Family legal matters such as divorce and inheritance are handled by Islamic *Sharia* courts. Non-Muslims are free to follow their own religious laws concerning family matters.

Adult children usually live with their parents until they are married. Even after marriage, young couples frequently live with one set of parents for some time. Widowed parents usually live with their children and their families. People of every age are expected to obey their parents and respect their wishes.

Families often keep strict watch on the activities of unmarried women. All women are expected to behave very carefully and modestly to ensure they maintain their reputations. A damaged reputation brings dishonor to a woman's family, especially its male members. Even if she does nothing to provoke him, a man can hurt a woman's reputation simply by the way he addresses her. In rural areas women participate in agricultural work. In the cities, only about one in ten women works outside the home. Many city women who work are educated professionals.

LEISURE

Men and women rarely interact outside the home. In cities, men frequent cafes where they can talk, drink strong Turkish coffee or tea, read newspapers, play board games, and smoke cigarettes or traditional water pipes called hookahs. Women do most of their socializing at home with other women. Soccer is popular among Syrian children; they play it more commonly as a street game than as an organized sport. Syrians also like to watch television and listen to the radio. Egyptian television programs and entertainers are especially popular. The government forbids individuals to use satellite dishes for television reception, but some people break this rule. Computers are very rare in Syria: only 1 percent of the population has access to the Internet.

The center of Syrian social life and leisure time is the home. In the cities, many people live in modern apartment buildings. In smaller towns and villages, Syrian homes are arranged with all the rooms opening onto a central courtyard, which is usually planted with a garden and sometimes fruit trees. Homes in older sections of the cities also follow this design.

Good hospitality is an important value of Syrian culture. Syrians are eager to open their homes to guests,

A Bedouin woman with tattoos on her face in Busayrah.

and mealtimes are often an important social occasion, lasting several hours. Hosting a successful get-together requires serving huge quantities of food. The entire table is often completely covered with dishes brimming with a vast array of choices. Guests are encouraged to eat as much as possible.

FASHION

Syrians wear a mix of Western and traditional clothing. In the cities, almost all the men wear the Western clothes common in Europe and the United States. They almost always wear long pants. Many women in the cities also wear Western-style clothes, but they usually dress conservatively. Loose-fitting clothing, long sleeves, and longer skirts are common, and Syrian women rarely wear pants.

It has long been traditional for Muslim women to cover their hair and faces with veils as a sign of modesty. This custom declined among modern Syrian women for a while, but wearing a head covering is becoming more popular again. Some view it as an outward sign of their Islamic faith. In the past, the secular government has discouraged women from wearing veils and head coverings in the past. Some devout Muslim women chose to wear a veil as a subtle form of protest against the government's interference.

Some women also feel less socially constrained in traditional clothing, with less concern for their safety and their reputations. Some professional women state that their male colleagues are more likely to treat them as equals when they wear concealing clothes. Very conservative Muslim women may wear veils that cover their faces, leaving only their eyes exposed. But more women choose to wear the *hijab*, a head scarf that covers the hair. The most popular fabric for the *hijab* in Syria is black silk. Many traditional ethnic costumes can still be seen around the Syrian countryside.

MINORITY GROUPS

While Syria is generally considered an Arab nation, Syria is also home to a number of smaller ethnic groups that make the country more diverse. The Kurds are a minority group living in Iraq, Iran, and Turkey as well as Syria. Syrian Kurds are Sunni Muslims who speak Kurdish. Most live on the northeastern steppes where they farm and herd sheep.

Armenians are a group mainly composed of Christians who tend to settle in cities. Some belong to the Armenian Orthodox Church and others to the Armenian Catholic Church. Circassians are Sunni Muslims who originally came from southern Russia. Many are village dwellers and farmers concentrated in the Hauran and Golan areas, though a large segment of those in the Golan Heights have moved to Damascus since Israel took over the region. Assyrians live east of the Euphrates. They consist primarily of Christians who belong to the Syrian Orthodox Church, also called the Jacobite Church.

In addition to Arabic, many educated Syrians speak either French or English. Kurds speak Kurdish, which is more closely related to European languages than to Middle Eastern languages. Armenians and Circassians have their own languages. Assyrians speak Syriac, a modern version of Aramaic. Most non-Arabs in Syria speak Arabic as well as their minority language. Some of these minority languages are mainly used in religious services and ceremonies.

In the past, many nomads roamed Syria's deserts and steppes. Most of these nomads were Bedouins, a traditional group of Muslims who spoke a very old form of Arabic and pursued an independent, nomadic lifestyle. Nomads traveled all year long, setting up camp wherever they found food for their camels and sheep. They lived in tents made of camel hair and survived on a diet of milk products and occasionally some meat. Although a small number of nomads still live in the desert, today most Bedouins live in cities and villages and lead a more settled lifestyle. Bedouins are still known for their independent spirit, and many Bedouin families enjoy returning to the desert for camel races and other activities that recall their heritage.

An aerial view of Damascus. The city in southwestern Syria is considered by many to be the oldest in the world, as Damascus was believed to have originally been settled between 8000 and 6000 B.C. Today, it is the capital of Syria.

Communities

With its ties to ancient civilizations, Syria is a fascinating destination for any serious student of ancient history and culture. Unfortunately, since 1979 Syria has been on the U.S. State Department's list of states that sponsor terrorism, and as a result many Westerners have been hesitant to cross the country's borders. While Syria is often associated with the widespread violence so familiar to the Middle East, a majority of visitors who have passed through its cities and countryside have reported that the Syrian citizens are friendly and welcoming.

Syria's coastline and mountain ranges attracted its early inhabitants as proper locations for their first major cities. Today, most of Syria's population lives in the western half of the country, with heavy concentrations in the cities of Damascus, Aleppo, and Latakia. These cities are considered some of the oldest in the world, though in modern times parts of them have been developed. About half of the country's population lives in rural areas, primarily in small village communities.

DAMASCUS

Damascus is Syria's capital and second-largest city. Many people believe it is the oldest surviving city in the world. The area of Damascus already contained settled inhabitants in 5000 B.C. It served as the capital of the province of Syria under the Roman Empire and later on, the capital of the Omayyad caliphs after the birth of Islam. Set in the foothills of the Anti-Lebanon Mountains, Damascus functioned as a "desert port" for the caravan routes of antiquity. It was the last place caravans traveling through southern Syria stopped before entering the desert, and the first place they reached upon leaving it.

The bustling Souk al-Hamidiye in Damascus.

Today, Damascus is a modern, growing center of government and business. The population of Damascus is growing rapidly as many people move there in search of education and opportunities not available in the country. In 2003, the city's population was estimated at 1,871,000 people.

Damascus is a place where the old and new intermingle. High-rise buildings and modern shopping districts contrast with old open-air markets known as souqs. It is the seat of a modern style of government, yet many buildings in Damascus date back to ancient times. In an effort to absorb the increasing numbers of people who have moved there in search of opportunity, the city has expanded into the nearby mountain slopes. Many of these mountain neighborhoods are overcrowded slums.

The residential suburbs and industrial areas that have grown up around Damascus' city center have helped cause traffic and more overcrowding. Although the older streets of Damascus tend to be narrow, several wide boulevards cross the center of town, with Martyrs' Square at its heart. These streets are lined with restaurants, shops, movie theaters, and hotels.

OTHER CITIES AND TOWNS

Aleppo is Syria's largest city, with a population estimated at 1,933,700 in 2003. The city grew along an ancient trade route linking Mediterranean ports to the Euphrates River, and it rivals Damascus as one of the world's oldest cities. Like Damascus, it formerly served as a "desert port." It was the last large urban center on the caravan route before travelers reached the long stretch of empty steppe and desert. No longer a center for trade, Aleppo is a major producer of textiles today. These products include silk and printed cotton fabric. Other industrial products include processed food products and leather made from the hides of animals pastured on the steppe.

An overview of Aleppo, Syria's largest city.

Homs is an industrial city located near the Orontes River and the Homs Gap. Its population was estimated at 751,500 in 2003, making it the third-largest city in Syria. Oil pipelines cross Homs on their way to the Homs Gap. Its location on these pipelines has made Homs an important center for oil refineries and petroleum distribution. The city has always been famous for silk making. Today, textiles are one of Homs' most important industries, with factories that produce silk, cotton, and rayon cloth. Sugar refineries process sugar beets, one of the major crops of the Orontes Valley. Factories take phosphate from the desert near Palmyra and turn it into fertilizer. A hydroelectric plant on the Orontes near Homs generates power for the city.

Hama lies north of Homs on the Orontes River. It is Syria's fifth-largest city with a population of 273,000 people in 1995. One of Syria's ancient caravan towns, Hama lies at the center of a fertile agricultural region, and its people tend to be conservative. For hundreds of years, the city was home to many of the powerful families who owned most of Syria's farmland. Today, most of Hama's citizens are Sunni Muslims, and they are known for their strict adherence to their religion. During the suppression of the Muslim Brotherhood uprising in 1982, the Syrian army destroyed entire sections of the city.

Hama is famous for its *norias*, huge wooden waterwheels that were once used to pump river water into pools and wells for drinking and irrigation. The smallest *norias* measure more than 30 feet (9 meters) across. Some *norias* are twice that size. *Norias* have been used to pump water in the Mediterranean region since ancient times.

Latakia, lying on the Mediterranean Sea, dates back to ancient times, and is famous for its large Alawi population. Qardaha, a nearby village, is the birthplace of Hafiz al-Assad and is considered

The city of Hama is famous for its ancient water wheels, or *norias*, on the Orontes River. Hama was also the site of protests and uprisings in 1964 and 1982.

Eid means "feast" or "festival." On Eid al-Fitr and Eid al-Adha, Muslims exchange the greeting "Eid Mubarak" (Blessed Eid).

the seat of Alawi power. Today, Latakia is the principal port on Syria's short coast. Almost all of Syria's imports and exports pass through Latakia. The government has put considerable investment into the city's infrastructure. A railroad connects Latakia to the Ghab Valley along the Orontes. Facilities at the port include docks, warehouses, refrigeration buildings, and a grain silo. Merchandise for import or export is processed at a customs house near the port. Passenger boats travel between Latakia and Alexandria, Egypt; Beirut, Lebanon; and the island of Cyprus. Latakia ranks as the fourth-largest city in Syria, with an estimated 417,100 people in 2003.

HOLIDAYS AND FESTIVALS

Syrians have quite a few government holidays when schools and businesses close. One of these is the national holiday, Evacuation Day, on April 17. Syrian Christians also celebrate Christmas and Easter. For Muslims, the most important celebrations of the year are the religious holidays of the Islamic calendar, which is based on the lunar months.

During the entire month of Ramadan, the ninth month of the Islamic calendar, Muslims are not permitted to eat or drink between sunrise and sunset. This fast, called *Sawm*, is the fourth pillar of Islam. Each evening during Ramadan families gather for a large meal after sunset, and say special prayers at this time. Muslims believe that this fasting purifies the body and strengthens the spirit.

Eid al-Fitr is a three-day celebration of the end of Ramadan. It begins on the first day of the tenth month of the Islamic calendar. It is a joyful time of celebration and thanksgiving for Allah's gifts, and fasting is forbidden. On the first morning of Eid al-Fitr, Muslims eat a large breakfast and wear their best clothing to the mosque to take part in morning prayers together. People often buy new clothes to wear for Eid al-Fitr and they get together for feasts and parties with their families and friends. Children receive gifts, money, and sweets from friends and relatives.

Many cities in Syria hold fireworks and street carnivals during Eid al-Fitr. Although the celebration lasts three days, Syrian shops and schools may close down for an entire week if the holiday falls in the middle of the week. As part of Zakat al-Fitr, a duty performed during the holiday, people also give gifts to charity.

The third pillar of Islam is the hajj, the pilgrimage to Mecca that every Muslim is supposed to undertake at least once. This pilgrimage takes place every year on the seventh to tenth days of the last month of the *Hijrah*. The rituals of the hajj include sacrificing a sheep on the final day. Many Muslims around the world participate in this custom, even when they are not in Mecca.

The celebration of the last day of the hajj is called Eid al-Adha. Those who can afford to sacrifice a sheep usually give one-third of the meat to the poor and one-third to friends and neighbors. They keep the final third for themselves and their families. This celebration is a time of feasting, prayer, and gift-giving. Schools and businesses close down for several days.

A young Syrian boy sits in the Golan Heights, near telephone poles on which the Syrian flag has been painted. This area of southwestern Syria has been occupied by Israel since 1967, and has added to tensions between the two countries.

Foreign Relations

Syria's main allies continue to be the other Arab states in the Middle East, although their relationships have been strained at times. Syrians have often expected other Arab states to follow their lead in their inflexible policy toward Israel. The close tie between Syria and Iran in the 1980s caused some friction with other Arab states. Syria has always promoted Arab unity, and broke relations with Egypt when it signed a treaty with Israel in 1979. Relations between Syria and Egypt were restored in 1989, the same year that Egypt was readmitted to the Arab League. Syria's relationship with the Persian Gulf states is generally good. Many Syrians work in these wealthy oil-producing countries, which have given Syria considerable economic aid.

Relations were strained with Jordan when it made peace with Israel in 1994. Although their fathers sometimes conflicted over the years, Bashar al-Assad and Jordan's new leader, King Abdullah, have a good relationship and have expressed a willingness to work together for the good of both countries. Jordan and Syria signed agreements to cooperate economically in 1999.

The relationship between Syria and Iraq has been more complicated. Their governments have been rivals, each believing its version of Baath Party philosophy to be the correct one. For years, disgruntled politicians from one country would seek exile in the other, as tensions grew hotter. Syria's support of Iran in its war against Iraq added to the hostility, and its participation in the Gulf War against Iraq further damaged Syrian-Iraqi relations. The two countries have frequently battled over the water rights of the Euphrates, as well as the management of the oil pipeline running from Iraq through Syria.

However, Syria and Iraq have been some steps made to improve their relations. Their international border, which was closed in 1980, has since been reopened. Travelers between the two countries no longer need visas, and trade between them has increased.

Since the Gulf War, the UN has imposed strict trade sanctions against Iraq. Saddam Hussein, Iraq's president, has repeatedly obstructed UN inspectors looking for nuclear, chemical, and biological weapons. The trade sanctions prohibit UN member states from purchasing oil from Iraq, though Iraq, which is plagued by poverty and famine, can get paid indirectly for its oil via the UN-sponsored oil-for-foods program.

Along with some other Arab countries, Syria has called for eliminating these sanctions and has stated that it does not support military attacks on Iraq. The Arab League denounced American and British air strikes on Iraq in 1998. Syria has reopened the Iraqi pipeline, and many people believe that Syria is buying oil from Iraq, helping its neighbor to get around the UN sanctions.

Ties are especially close between the governments of Syria and

Lebanon for the simple reason that Syrian troops have had a long history of occupation there. Syria exerts a great deal of control over the Lebanese government. Lebanon is strategically important to Syria in its opposition to Israel. Syria has provided financial and military support for Hezbollah, a militant Shiite group operating within Lebanon that commits terrorist acts against Israel. By attacking from Lebanon, these terrorists help deflect criticism away from Syria. The Lebanese Muslim leadership has relied on Syrian forces for security, but Lebanese Christians have always objected to their presence.

Egypt and Syria had close ties, and twice formed pan-Arab associations (the United Arab Republic from 1958 to 1961 and the Federation of Arab Republics, which also included Libya, from 1972 to 1977). However, when Egyptian president Anwar el-Sadat signed a peace agreement with Israel, Syria angrily broke off relations with Egypt. Pictured are Sadat (left), Israeli prime minister Menachem Begin (right), and U.S. president Jimmy Carter, who had helped negotiate the peace agreement at Camp David in September 1978.

Syria was involved in negotiating the Taif Accord, which called for the withdrawal of Syrian forces by 1992. The accord also contains a section on relations between Syria and Lebanon that led to the Syria-Lebanon Cooperation Treaty in 1991. This treaty asserts that Syria and Lebanon are two separate independent states but also acknowledges their close ties. In reality, Syria has not treated Lebanon as a truly separate and independent nation. The two countries do not have embassies on one another's soil, and they have established no formal diplomatic relations despite the extremely close contact between their governments. It is if they are two states sharing one country.

Since the Israeli withdrawal from southern Lebanon in 2000, the rationale for Syria's continued military presence in Lebanon has disappeared. Lebanese calls for Syrian withdrawal and fulfillment of the Taif Accord are becoming stronger and more frequent. The Lebanese people favor true independence. Syria's troops have moved further back to their own border, but they are still stationed in Lebanon.

Relations between Syria under Hafiz al-Assad and the Palestinian Liberation Organization (PLO) were always cold. PLO chairman Yasir Arafat sought help from Arab countries but often acted independently without consulting other Arabs about policy decisions. Assad did not want an ally he could not easily control, especially since Palestinian attacks on Israel have often brought Israeli retaliation against Arab countries.

The Syrian government became particularly angry with Arafat when he began to negotiate one-on-one with Israel without involving other Arab countries in the peace process. Arafat's actions went against Syria's firm stance that the Arabs should negotiate with Israel as a collective unit. Syria has sheltered and funded Palestinian groups that are hostile to Arafat. Most of these groups still believe that Israel has no right to exist and are angry because

Arafat has recognized Israel and at least played at negotiating for peace. Terrorist attacks by these Palestinian opposition groups have hampered Arafat's relations with Israel and the United States and placed major roadblocks in the peace process.

The peace process with Israel has broken down, and relations between Bashar al-Assad and Arafat, now president of the Palestinian Authority, are warming. Arafat attended the funeral of Assad's father in 2000. Assad and Arafat met again at the Arab Summit in Amman, Jordan, in March 2001, and discussed the peace process. Now that Egypt and Jordan are at peace with Israel, Assad keenly desires a united front composed of Syria, Lebanon, and the Palestinian Authority to negotiate terms with Israel.

Assad has also stated that the violent Palestinian uprising against Israel should continue. In the past, Arafat has occasionally worked to quell violence to smooth relations with Israel and the United States. His relationships with these countries have gone sour, and he appears more willing to try Syria's approach. Syria has never recognized the statehood of the Palestinian Authority, but is now making moves in that direction. People holding Palestinian Authority passports are now allowed entry into Syria, and there is talk of opening a Palestinian embassy in Damascus.

ISRAEL

Syria has consistently been the most hostile and bitter of all Israel's Arab neighbors. Other countries have made advances in the peace process: Lebanon agreed with Israel on a permanent international boundary, and Egypt and Jordan both agreed on borders with Israel. Syria, however, refuses to accept Israel's occupation of the Golan Heights. The Israeli parliament voted to apply Israeli laws to the Golan Heights in 1981. Syria has encouraged and aided groups responsible for numerous terrorist attacks on Israeli soil. These groups include Hezbollah, Hamas, and the

An army jeep, and other items left behind after Israel's May 2000 withdrawal from its buffer zone in southern Lebanon, are burned by Lebanese happy to see the Israelis gone. Although after the Israeli pullout there was no reason for Syria to keep troops in Lebanon, thousands of Syrian soldiers remain.

Abu Nidal organization.

Negotiations to establish peace between Syria and Israel have failed on two counts. Syria refuses to make peace with Israel until all Arab countries make peace, including the Palestinians. Syria also demands the immediate return of the entire Golan Heights up to the 1967 border as a requirement for peace. Israel has not agreed to either of these conditions. It is particularly concerned because one-third of its water supply originates in the Golan Heights. It wants guarantees from Syria that this supply will not be interrupted. The two countries also disagree on the timing of future actions. Israel wants peace and normal relations before it will withdraw from the Golan Heights, and it wants to withdraw gradually, moving the border back one step at a time. Syria wants the entire Golan returned immediately and will not recognize Israel or establish relations until the withdrawal is accomplished.

TURKEY AND IRAN

Water rights are Syria's largest issue with Turkey. Turkish dams have the power to severely restrict the amount of water reaching Syria in the Euphrates River. Another matter of serious concern for Syria is the increasingly close relationship between Turkey and Israel. The two countries signed a military cooperation agreement in 1995 and a free trade agreement in 1996. They have participated in naval training exercises in the Mediterranean in which the United States was involved.

Turkey and Israel have also discussed water projects to transport water from Turkey to Israel. Syria's fear is that Turkey will divert water sources from Syria in order to send water to Israel. With Turkey to the north cooperating with the enemy Israel to the south, Syria finds itself in a vulnerable situation. This is one possible factor behind Syria's recent reconciliation with Iraq in order to gain some support.

Syrians continue to consider the Turkish Hatay province a part of their territory and resent the Turks for taking it in 1939. The Kurdistan Workers Party (PKK) is a Kurdish group that has been trying to separate from Turkey since 1984. The party has committed terrorist acts in Turkey to further this aim. Several of the group's leaders had been hiding in the Kurdish area of Syria in the 1990s. Syria expelled them in 1998, which helped to improve relations between the two countries.

Toward the end of the 1980s, Syria's friendly relations with Iran began to disintegrate. Closer cooperation with Iraq could cool relations with Iran even more. A fundamentalist Muslim state, Iran opposes any peace with Israel and was alarmed by Syrian attempts at reconciliation in the 1990s.

RELATIONS WITH THE WEST

The ties between Syria and Europe are mainly economic. Syria's relationships with European nations have been somewhat friendly in recent years. Bashar al-Assad is working toward closer ties with the European Union (EU) because Syria needs the economic assistance that Europe can provide. Syria sells most of its exports to West European countries and buys most of its imports from them as well. The EU has been giving Syria financial assistance since 1977. Syria has borrowed funds from European banks, and the EU has provided money for specific improvement projects in Syria. The slight liberalization of Syria's economic policies in recent years may help EU nations to feel more comfortable with the business climate in Syria.

The United States has been extremely involved in Middle Eastern affairs, most often as a staunch ally of Israel. The U.S. government has given Israel money, weapons, and military equipment and has viewed Israel as an ally for most of the country's troubled history, especially since 1967. In addition, many American Jews have helped Israel financially. As a result of this support, many Arabs view the United States with suspicion and resentment.

For the United States, the biggest obstacle to good relations with Syria is its sponsorship of terrorism. Following the September 2001 terrorist attacks on the World Trade Center in New York and the Pentagon in Washington, D.C., Syria's role in international terrorism became an even greater concern than before. In 2003, Syria remained on the U.S. State Department's list of states that sponsor terrorism. Syria has not been directly linked to any terrorist acts since 1986, and it has made an effort to stop terrorists from launching attacks from Syrian soil. It also does not directly support terrorist attacks on Westerners. But several Palestinian opposition groups still have their headquarters in Damascus. The Syrian government has said it will expel proven terrorists from the country, though the U.S. State Department remains unconvinced.

The most threatening terrorist organizations with Syrian ties are those based beyond Syria's borders. Two infamous groups, Hezbollah and Hamas, operate from the Bekaa Valley in Lebanon with no interference from the Syrian troops that are stationed

Syrian president Bashar al-Assad walks with King Abdullah II of Jordan. The two leaders were on their way to a March 2001 summit of the Arab League.

there. The Bekaa Valley is near Lebanon's Syrian border. The Syrians do not classify Hezbollah and Hamas as terrorists. Instead, they claim that these groups are freedom fighters resisting Israeli occupation of their country. These groups often attack civilians, however, and these attacks have aggravated tension between Israel and the Palestinian Authority and have held back the peace process. In April 2002, after Hezbollah fighters in Lebanon launched missile attacks into disputed territory in Lebanon, U.S. Secretary of State Colin Powell visited Beirut and Damascus to help mediate. Powell received assurances from President Assad that Syria would do what it could to control Hezbollah.

Because Syria sponsors terrorism, and its government denies certain civil rights to its citizens, the United States has imposed sanctions on the country. It will not sell weapons to Syria, offer economic aid, or buy most Syrian products. It is also believed that Syria may have a supply of chemical and biological weapons, which gives the United States one additional reason to keep the sanctions in place.

For Syria, the United States' close relationship with Israel has prevented friendly relations. Syrians believe that the United States is biased toward Israel, holding it to a different standard than it does the Arabs. Anti-American feeling has been exhibited by the Syrian people most pointedly after Israeli attacks on Palestinian settlements.

There have been some recent steps toward cooperation between Syria and the United States. After the terrorist attacks on the World Trade Center and the Pentagon, Assad sent a letter to President Bush expressing his sympathy. He also stated Syria's willingness to help the United States track down terrorists. There is evidence that Syria has helped the CIA to locate Muslim fundamentalist terrorists hiding in Europe. However, the Syrian government's problems with its terrorist associates in Lebanon remain unsolved. In the years ahead, terrorist attacks against Israeli sites remain a constant threat as long as Syria and other Arab states maintain their ties with groups like Hezbollah and Hamas. Because Syria is a country ever committed to Arab unity, it is clear that Arab disputes with Israel will most likely remain Syrian disputes, and vice versa.

CHRONOLOGY

3000 B.C.: Damascus and Aleppo are settled.

4th century B.C.: Alexander the Great invades Syria and the Middle East.

62 B.C.: The Roman general Pompey invades and claims Syria for Rome.

A.D. 33: Christianity is founded.

330: Constantine moves the capital of the Roman Empire to Constantinople.

622: Muhammad and his followers move from Mecca to Medina; the first year of the Muslim calendar, also called the first year of the *Hijrah*.

635: Damascus falls to the Muslim conquerors.

636: Arab Muslims defeat the Byzantines at the Battle of Yarmouk in Syria.

7th century: The Omayyad caliphate rules from Damascus; Islam spreads across North Africa to Spain and east to western India.

8th century: The Abbasid caliphs replace the Omayyads and move the capital to Baghdad.

1055: The Turks capture Baghdad and its leader is named sultan.

11th to 13th centuries: Christian crusaders from Europe occupy fortresses near the Syrian coast.

1260: Mongols invade Syria and destroy much of Damascus and Aleppo.

1453: Ottoman Turks capture Constantinople.

1516: Ottoman Turks capture Syria.

1529: Sultan Suleyman the Magnificent attacks Vienna but fails to capture it.

1683: Another unsuccessful attack on Vienna leads to final defeat for the Ottomans; they are forced to sign a peace treaty.

1909: Jewish settlers in Palestine build the city of Tel Aviv.

1914: The Ottomans join World War I in alliance with the Germans.

1916: Britain and France sign the Sykes-Picot agreement, determining to divide Syria at the end of the war.

1917: Under the Balfour Declaration, the British declare their support for a Jewish national state.

1918: The British and Arabs capture Damascus.

1920: The French army marches on Damascus; the French occupation begins.

1928: The Nationalist Bloc forms in Syria.

CHRONOLOGY

1938: World War II begins.

1939: France gives to Turkey the province of Alexandretta, which is renamed the province of Hatay.

1940: France surrenders to Nazi Germany; Vichy France governs Syria.

1943: Syrian nationalists declare the end of the French mandate.

1945: Syria enters World War II on the side of the Allies; joins the Arab League.

1946: French troops evacuate Syria on April 17.

1947: The Baath Party officially incorporates in Syria.

1948: The State of Israel is created; the first Arab-Israeli war begins.

1949: The armistice agreement with Israel gives the land north of Lake Tiberias to Syria.

1954: Parliament and the Syrian constitution are restored after a series of military coups.

1958: Parliament, led by the majority Baath Party, votes to unite with Egypt and create the United Arab Republic, which lasts only three years.

1963: A military coup is led by a coalition of military officers, many with ties to the Baath Party.

1964: The Palestinian Liberation Organization (PLO) is organized and makes initial demands for Palestinian statehood.

1965: Syria's government assumes ownership of many businesses.

1966: Salah Jadid, a military officer and radical socialist member of Baath, takes over the government in another coup.

1967: Arab countries wage second war with Israel; Israel wins control of the Golan Heights and the Sinai Peninsula; the United Nations Security Council passes Resolution 242, which demands Israel return territories won in the war; Israel doesn't comply after failed peace negotiations with Arab countries.

1970: Jordan expels the PLO, which moves its headquarters to Lebanon; Syrian military enters Lebanon and fights alongside the PLO in civil war; Hafiz al-Assad, Jadid's Minister of Defense, seizes power in a bloodless coup.

1971: Assad becomes president of Syria in a national referendum.

1973: A Syrian constitution is drafted, giving enormous power to the president and the Baath Party; Egypt and Syria go to war with Israel.

CHRONOLOGY

1976: Civil war breaks out in Lebanon between Maronite Christians and Shiite Muslims; Syria sends troops to support the Shiites.

1979: Egypt and Israel sign a peace agreement; the Arab League withdraws Egypt's membership.

1982: Israel invades Lebanon; the Syrian military attacks the city of Hama to end the Muslim Brotherhood uprising, killing as many as 25,000 people.

1989: The Lebanese Parliament negotiates the Taif Accord, an agreement designed to restore peace and government in Lebanon; the Arab League readmits Egypt, and Syria restores relations with Egypt.

1990: Syria joins a coalition of countries fighting against Iraq in the Gulf War.

1991: Syria attends a Middle East peace conference in Madrid.

1993: Israel and the PLO sign a peace agreement in Oslo, Norway.

1996: Israel gives the Palestinian National Authority limited power and independence to rule Palestinians in the West Bank and the Gaza Strip.

2000: Syria and Israel break off peace negotiations in January; in May, Israeli troops pull out of southern Lebanon; Hafiz al-Assad dies in June, and his son Bashar takes his place.

2001: Bashar al-Assad and Yasir Arafat meet privately in March at an Arab summit to discuss terms for peace with Israel; in June, most of Syria's troops pull out of Beirut.

2002: In March, the Arab League endorses a peace initiative proposed by Crown Prince Abdullah of Saudi Arabia; Syrian troops in Lebanon move back to the Bekaa Valley in April.

2003: In January, Syria meets with Turkey and Arab nations to discuss ways to avoid involvement in expected U.S.-Iraq war; in February, the Syrian military dismantles several of its bases in northern Lebanon and moves troops out of the area.

GLOSSARY

armistice—an agreement between two warring parties to stop fighting.

caliph—the title of a successor of Muhammad as the spiritual and political leader of Islam.

caravan—a train of pack animals carrying cargo from one place to another.

coup—short for coup d'etat, the sudden illegal overthrow of one government for another, usually by means of force.

diplomatic relations—a relationship between two countries in which each agrees to acknowledge the independent statehood of the other and establish ties through government representatives known as diplomats.

embassy—the official headquarters of an ambassador and his or her staff.

exports—goods that are sold to other countries.

gross domestic product (GDP)—the total value of goods and services produced within a nation in a given year.

gross domestic product per capita—the gross domestic product divided by the total number of people living in a nation.

hajj—a pilgrimage to Mecca required of all Muslims.

imams—leaders of prayer in a Muslim mosque, also those descendents of Muhammad's cousin Ali believed by Shiite Muslims to be Islam's legitimate rulers.

irrigation—the process of bringing water to an agricultural land from a distant water source via canals and ditches.

League of Nations—an organization of nations that lasted from 1920 to 1946.

mandates—orders to act that are given to representatives; specifically the authority given by the League of Nations that its member nations administer and establish a government on a conquered territory.

martial law—law that is enforced by military power, usually in a state of emergency when the civilian government is unable to keep order

monotheism—belief in the existence of only one God.

Pan-Arabism—a philosophy that loyalty to Arabs and an Arab identity takes precedence over loyalty to an individual nation or tribe.

Qur'an—the book containing the sacred writings of the Muslims, which they believe is the word of Allah dictated to Muhammad by the angel Gabriel.

GLOSSARY

Ramadan—the ninth month of the Islamic calendar, when Muslims fast and pray to commemorate the appearance of the angel Gabriel to the prophet Muhammad.

Semites—people of the Eastern Mediterranean area descended from its original Semitic tribes, including Jews and Arabs.

Sharia—Islamic law based on the Qur'an and the *Sunna*.

Shiites—followers of the main minority sect of Islam who consider descendents of Ali the rightful heirs of Muhammad.

steppe—level, treeless, grassy plains with low rainfall, found in eastern Europe and Asia.

Sunnis—those comprising the majority sect of Islam that accepts the first four caliphs as heirs of Muhammad.

Sunna—Muslim law based on the words and actions of Muhammad.

Zionism—an international movement that lobbied for an independent Jewish state and since 1948, has supported Israel.

FURTHER READING

Ball, Warwick. *Syria: A Historical and Architectural Guide*. New York: Interlink Books, 1998.

Batatu, Hanna. *Syria's Peasantry, the Descendants of Its Lesser Notables, and Their Politics*. Princeton, N.J.: Princeton University Press, 1999.

Burns, Ross. *Monuments of Syria: An Historical Guide*. London: I.B. Tauris, 1999.

Davis, Scott C. *The Road from Damascus: A Journey Through Syria*. Seattle, Wash.: Cune Press, 2003.

Fromkin, David. *A Peace to End All Peace*. New York: Henry Holt, 1989.

Joris, Lieve. *The Gates of Damascus*. Melbourne, Aus.: Lonely Planet Publications, 1996.

Lewis, Bernard. *The Middle East: A Brief History of the Last 2,000 Years*, trans. Sam Garrett. New York: Scribner, 1995.

Seale, Patrick. *Asad of Syria: The Struggle for the Middle East*. Berkley: University of California Press, 1988 (revised 1995).

http://memory.loc.gov/frd/cs/sytoc.html

This site provides an organized introduction to the geography, history, politics, and economy of Syria.

www.cia.gov/cia/publications/factbook/geos/sy.html

An up-to-date fact sheet on Syria provided by the CIA. Includes map of the country.

www.syriatourism.org

The official site of the Ministry of Tourism. This site is hard to navigate and under construction, but it has extensive information about Syria's cities and countryside.

www.lonelyplanet.com/destinations/middle_east/syria

An informative tourist site published by Lonely Planet Guides. It includes a slide show of Syria's tourist attractions.

www.syriagate.com

This Syrian website is a great resource for general information about the country. There are dozens of links to other useful websites, including some of major government organizations.

www.mideasti.org

An extensive resource geared to educate Americans about the Middle East. This academic site includes loads of information for research.

www.mideastweb.org.

This site is maintained by a non-profit Israeli organization and contains essays and discussions about the most recent issues and events in the Middle East.

INDEX

Numbers in **bold italic** refer to captions.

INDEX

INDEX

PICTURE CREDITS

CONTRIBUTORS

The **FOREIGN POLICY RESEARCH INSTITUTE (FPRI)** served as editorial consultants for the MODERN MIDDLE EAST NATIONS series. FPRI is one of the nation's oldest "think tanks." The Institute's Middle East Program focuses on Gulf security, monitors the Arab-Israeli peace process, and sponsors an annual conference for teachers on the Middle East, plus periodic briefings on key developments in the region.

Among the FPRI's trustees is a former Secretary of State and a former Secretary of the Navy (and among the FPRI's former trustees and interns, two current Undersecretaries of Defense), not to mention two university presidents emeritus, a foundation president, and several active or retired corporate CEOs.

The scholars of FPRI include a former aide to three U.S. Secretaries of State, a Pulitzer Prize–winning historian, a former president of Swarthmore College and a Bancroft Prize–winning historian, and two former staff members of the National Security Council. And the FPRI counts among its extended network of scholars—especially its Inter-University Study Groups—representatives of diverse disciplines, including political science, history, economics, law, management, religion, sociology, and psychology.

DR. HARVEY SICHERMAN is president and director of the Foreign Policy Research Institute in Philadelphia, Pennsylvania. He has extensive experience in writing, research, and analysis of U.S. foreign and national security policy, both in government and out. He served as Special Assistant to Secretary of State Alexander M. Haig Jr. and as a member of the Policy Planning Staff of Secretary of State James A. Baker III. Dr. Sicherman was also a consultant to Secretary of the Navy John F. Lehman Jr. (1982–1987) and Secretary of State George Shultz (1988).

A graduate of the University of Scranton (B.S., History, 1966), Dr. Sicherman earned his Ph.D. at the University of Pennsylvania (Political Science, 1971), where he received a Salvatori Fellowship. He is author or editor of numerous books and articles, including *America the Vulnerable: Our Military Problems and How to Fix Them* (FPRI, 2002) and *Palestinian Autonomy, Self-Government and Peace* (Westview Press, 1993). He edits *Peacefacts*, an FPRI bulletin that monitors the Arab-Israeli peace process.

ANNE MARIE SULLIVAN received her Bachelor of Arts degree from Temple University and has worked in the publishing industry as a writer and editor. She lives in suburban Philadelphia with her husband and three children. This is her second book for school students.